Jim Walden's

TALES FROM THE WASHINGTON STATE COUGARS SIDELINE

JIM WALDEN
WITH
DAVE BOLING

Sports Publishing L.L.C.
www.SportsPublishingLLC.com

Director of production: Susan M. Moyer
Acquisitions editor: Dean Reinke
Developmental editor: Regina D. Sabbia
Photo editor: Erin Linden-Levy
Project manager: Greg Hickman
Copy editor: Cynthia L. McNew
Dust jacket design: Joseph Brumleve
Imaging: Kenneth J. O'Brien
Marketing manager: Nick Obradovich

ISBN: 1-58261-256-0

Printed in the United States

All these experiences and stories were part of a wonderful 10-year period in a 31-year career in a profession I loved. To have as much fun as I did, you absolutely must have a great wife to support, share, encourage, and appreciate your profession as much as you do. Janice has always been all of that to me. She accepted prime responsibility for raising our children, each of whom I love dearly. They were taught to be themselves and not to be identified by their father's role as a coach. To have a great family and a job that you love is as good as it gets. This book is dedicated to that family, which made it all possible.

CONTENTS

ACKNOWLEDGMENTS

No coach ever has any measure of success without the help of others. I will always be indebted to the wonderful assistant coaches, secretaries, support staff and administrators I had. Just as important are your close and trusted friends who, win or lose, are always there. Those good friends in Pullman are still with us today. The major acknowledgment for this project goes to Dave Boling, who organized my ramblings and stories into this book, which I hope will bring some enjoyment to those who read it.

—Jim Walden

Many thanks are due to my family (for all the patient support), to Sports Publishing L.L.C. (for the opportunity), to the Washington State sports information department (for gracious assistance), and to the voluble and hilarious Jim Walden (for all the stories).

—Dave Boling

CHAPTER 1

HELLO, PULLMAN

KEPT IN THE DARK

I wish I could provide more insights into my first impressions of Pullman and Washington State University, and the unique landscapes that surround them. But I can't elaborate because I was a Cougar coach for more than a week before I ever saw the town by the light of day.

Warren Powers and I had previously coached together as assistants on some great Nebraska teams. When he got the Washington State head coaching job, he invited me to leave the University of Miami and come up to run the offense and assist with the Cougar quarterbacks. I spent a long day flying a diagonal across the country on January 3, 1977, dragged in at about 8 p.m., and was taken straight to Bohler Gym and tossed into a staff meeting.

So many of the other assistants had ties to Nebraska, too, so it felt like a homecoming for me. That first meeting went until well after midnight before they shuttled me over to a little two-bedroom place they rented for some of us over at the Steptoe Apartments. Real luxury all the way, I can tell you. There were four of us crammed in there for that entire semester. Dick Beechner and I were the older married guys, and they put us in with a couple of young, single guys, Richie Glover and Dave Redding. Richie was an All-American and Outland Trophy-winning defensive lineman, and Dave was another former Nebraska lineman. Dick and I, apparently, were their unofficial chaperones.

Beechner and I bunked in one room and let the young guys stay together in the other. It didn't take a genius to realize that those guys, who were in their 20s, weren't interested in just studying playbooks if they had some free time. Beechner and I weren't always sure what we were going to find when we opened that apartment door. Let's just say that sometimes we'd hear voices in there that were quite a bit higher than you'd expect from Richie Glover.

That first night, I got to bed at maybe 1 a.m. and had to be gone for a 5:30 a.m. flight to northern California for an extended recruiting trip. People sometimes talk about having to hit the ground running, but I barely had time to hit the ground at all. Warren had given me the whole East Bay area to recruit, and I don't think he realized there were about a million schools there. Well, I was off for a week selling Washington State University and Pullman to a bunch of kids and I hadn't even seen the town in the daylight.

But I very sincerely told them all what a wonderful place it was. What was I going to say? You'll love Pullman... it's really dark.

JACK THOMPSON

You could listen to Jack Thompson play quarterback. Only two passers I've ever been around—Jack Thompson and John Elway—threw the ball so hard that you could hear it sizzle as it cut through the air. I was astonished by the way the ball would whistle through the wind. Trust me, that's throwing it hard.

I was Jack's quarterback coach when I got to Pullman in 1977, and then his head coach the next year. Jack had a lot to do with me getting that job, in fact; he was a great ally. I know for a fact that Jack made a nice appeal to athletic director Sam Jankovich to hire me as head coach, and I think his support carried some weight.

Jack previously had been coached by Jackie Sherrill, who wanted to throw the ball on every play. Jack loved that, of course. But that wasn't the offense we were going to run. So, it took a while to wean him off the pass-first mindset. Jack made it easy, though, because he was such a tremendous guy and gifted quarterback.

Jack had only one shortcoming that sometimes got him in trouble. He was so confident in his ability that he would try to throw the ball through anything, including defenders' bodies. A lot of the great quarterbacks are guilty of this. Sometimes I'd get mad at him about it, but you're crazy as a coach if you try to challenge somebody's inner belief. Besides, he got away with it most of the time, because he could throw it so hard. A number of times I saw Jack zing a ball under the armpit of a defensive back who was sure he was in position for an interception.

Another thing that really helped Jack was the receivers he had: Bevan Maxey, Bob Bratkowski, Mike Levenseller and Brian Kelly. Those were four very special college receivers, and

Jack Thompson, the "Throwin' Samoan," left WSU as the most prolific passer in NCAA history. He was a fabulous leader with an arm so powerful the ball whistled as it flew. Even I wasn't silly enough to try to make him run the option... more than a few times, that is. (Photo courtesy of Washington State University)

they could really spoil you. They were very well coached and well prepared by the previous staff.

Jack was considered a Heisman Trophy candidate, although I knew he'd never get it, because we simply didn't have enough national clout at Washington State. But his numbers were right up there, and he certainly deserved the consideration. Aside from being so talented, he was a delightful guy, always upbeat. I was never one to baby my quarterbacks, but Jack never pouted and always handled it well. He understood my personality and accepted it.

THROWIN' SAMOAN

In his first game with our new staff, Jack Thompson was tossed into a cauldron… taking on Nebraska at Lincoln. I had seen how good he was, and how well the receivers complemented his talents, and while I may have been one of a small group of believers, I was convinced we could upset Nebraska.

We had scouted them so hard, trying to decode tendencies to gain any advantage. What we discovered was a habit of coming at opponents on all-out blitzes on first down whenever a team got inside their 20. The theory was to disrupt you and push you back out of field-goal range.

We felt that Jack could burn them on post routes against that blitz, and he threw a pair of touchdowns in that situation to Brian Kelly. We stunned them, 19-10. Jack was so cool and so exceptional; it was his first game with us, and he was everything you could ever ask for.

EARLY DEFECTOR

Opening against Nebraska in 1977 was strange because so many members of our Cougar staff had Nebraska ties, and so many on the Nebraska staff had worked with us. It was old-home week. But it got downright weird before the game even started.

It seems to me that we were wearing white jerseys and crimson pants and Nebraska had on the red jerseys and white pants; whatever it was, we had a very similar color scheme. That might have been at the root of the strangest pregame warm-up incident I've ever seen.

We had a young guy out of Lewiston, Idaho, named Steve Kalinoski. For whatever reason—perhaps he was getting extra taping or treatment—he came onto the field after the rest of the team. As a kid who is late will do, he hurried to where players were stretching and jumped in at the back of the line and started stretching along with them.

One problem, he joined in with the Cornhuskers.

You've got to understand, when fans go to Nebraska games, they may start tailgating at 9 a.m., but at noon, an hour before kickoff, they're in that stadium and watching. It didn't take long before both coaching staffs and everybody in the stands realized there's this Cougar in there warming up with Nebraska's guys. Everybody noticed it but Steve Kalinoski.

We didn't know what to do; nobody wanted to go down there and get him for fear of mortally embarrassing the kid. But right away I see John Melton, an old friend of mine on the Nebraska staff, heading over to me. I knew he had some wisecrack he was going to nail me with.

"So, do your Cougars think they've have got a chance against us today?"

Yeah, I think they do.

"Doesn't look like the sentiment is unanimous... one of your guys has defected over to our side before the game even started. Ol' No. 73 looks like he wants to play for us."

I think Warren Powers eventually sent a trainer down to get Steve. But I'm not sure Steve ever got over it; I think he quit the team the next year. But we won that Nebraska game, so I assume he was glad he finally came back over to our side.

JACK BE NIMBLE

Jack Thompson was never anybody's idea of a prototypical option quarterback. He had a big lower body and was clearly a classic drop-back, pocket passer. Although on at least one play he was better in the open field than anybody would have expected. We turned him loose against Arizona State in 1978, my third game as a head coach, and Jack torched the Sun Devils.

Jack had thrown touchdown pass after touchdown pass. Late in the game, we were at about their 25 when we called an option. Jack faked to the dive back and came down the line as their defender came upfield to take away the pitch back. The defender committed to the back because he knew that Jack wouldn't hurt them with the keeper.

But when Jack turned, there was absolutely nothing but green grass and white stripes in front of him. He turned it up and went uncontested to the end zone. He was just lumbering along like a big ol' Clydesdale, but I know in his mind he was bouncing like a gazelle.

He came off to the sidelines with a look of greater delight than I ever saw after he threw a touchdown pass. "Coach," he said. "This option stuff isn't so bad after all."

DAN DOORNINK

Dan Doornink, one of the better pass-receiving backs to play the game, exploited a unique attribute to his benefit: His voice. This is not one of those so-called measurable qualities that gets tested at combines, but it helped Danny all the way to the NFL.

He loved to catch passes, and he made a living in the National Football League by being able to find open spots under the coverage for the dump-off toss. Jack Thompson, of course, preferred throwing the ball deep downfield. But Danny would run these little circle routes, and when he got open, he'd scream "JAACCCKKKKK!" in this high, nasal voice that he had. I'll tell you, it got the quarterback's attention because that voice could penetrate your brain. It was a shrill sound, like some kind of wild parrot, and Jack would hear that and throw him the ball... maybe just to make the racket stop. But Danny would always catch it and turn it up field and get 12 yards on it.

Dan was a great student of the game; he understood the passing game and he stayed in the NFL for a long time because he really knew how to get open. And he certainly knew how to get a quarterback—and everybody else in shouting range—to look in his direction.

APPLE CUP '77: ICE BOWL

The biggest thing that came from the 1977 Apple Cup in Seattle was this: After a long, frozen afternoon, I was never going to take any crap from the University of Washington people about the weather being so bad in Pullman. It rained and froze solid the night before, and the part of the field that was shaded by the south stands never thawed out. Two-thirds of the field was like playing on an ice rink. The field was so hard that running back Mike Washington suffered a broken jaw when he was tackled to the frozen turf.

A lot of fans thought this was going to be a quarterback duel between Husky Warren Moon and our Jack Thompson— two of the great players to highlight this rivalry. But it was mostly controlled by their big ol' back named Joe Steele. He was one of their great players, whom I always likened favorably to the great USC I-backs. He was a guy with good natural traction who could run flatfooted on that ice, and we never could tackle him. Steele scored three touchdowns, two on passes from Moon, and they got up on us quickly with 21 points in the first quarter.

We were never really in the game after that, of course, as it was nearly impossible to claw back against a defense with linebacker Michael Jackson making 23 tackles.

The Huskies hadn't been to the Rose Bowl since 1963, and this was their first time going back. They clearly deserved it. But man, that day was horrible: Three hours of freezing rain running down the back of your neck. After that, I never had much patience for the UW people and their ongoing hysteria about how much Pullman resembles Nome, Alaska.

WONDERFUL KIDS, WEAK COACHING

I don't know if I ever enjoyed a group of better kids than that '77 Cougar bunch when I was an assistant. There were so many wonderful and diverse personalities, like Dan Doornink and Dean Pedigo, guys who just loved to practice and have fun. The secondary was the greatest collection of athletes at those positions I'd ever been around.

But we finished a marginal 6-5 that year, which was bumped to 7-4 after the UCLA loss was ruled a forfeit in our favor. It's a shame, because that was a team with eight-win talent that we coached down to six wins. As a staff, we were green and didn't know enough about what we were doing. There were a lot of coaching errors.

We opened with wins at Nebraska and Michigan State, but we blew the Kansas game (14-12 loss) when we had about 600 yards of offense and got only four field goals out of it. Then we lost the Stanford game (31-29), too.

We hadn't been together long as a staff and we didn't know how to establish a good plan every week, we didn't know how to fit the players to the plan, and we didn't know enough about the league. That was a great group of athletes that will always be very special to me. You might not hear a coach admit this much, but, sadly, they were better players than we were coaches. They deserved more from us.

POWERS OUTAGE

Sometimes you hear things you simply don't want to believe are true. About two-thirds of the way through the 1977 season, unsettling rumors started floating around the campus. It was being whispered that Cougar head coach Warren Powers was in the hunt to take over the job at Missouri. Although this would create the most important opportunity of my career, it just tore at my heart.

I loved Warren, but when there was a week or two left in that season, he told me he was going to leave to take the Missouri job, and it strained our friendship from that point. I felt I had no choice but to honestly and straightforwardly come out and tell him I didn't think it was the right thing to do. He had been the third head coach in three years at Washington State, and I knew he had promised the administration that he would be here for a while. I told him it was wrong, and he very obviously didn't like hearing that.

From my perspective, it was personal, and I guess there was a little hardheadedness involved, too. I was about to buy a house because we really loved Pullman. My wife Janice and I both grew up in small towns, and Pullman fit what we were looking for in a lifestyle. Warren warned me not to buy the house because he was ready to move the staff to Missouri.

Now, I had already been an assistant at Nebraska, where we had won two national championships and four conference championships. Why would I want to go back as an assistant to another school in that conference? Been there, done that. Done it better, in fact.

Once I told Warren exactly what I thought of his bailing out so soon, it was clear I wouldn't be wanted on his Missouri staff anymore. So, the best choice I had, since I had promised my kids I wasn't going to uproot them, was to get the head coaching position at WSU.

Athletic director Sam Jankovich interviewed three of us, Dick Beechner, Mike Price, and me. I felt I had a really good shot at it because I was the only one of the three who had coached in Division I on both sides of the ball. I had been at Nebraska under Bob Devaney and also the University of Miami. Dick had good credentials and surely deserved consideration. Mike was probably the dark horse because he hadn't been at it as long.

Thankfully, I got the job, and it turned out to be the best thing that ever happened to me. But to this day, I still think it was wrong of Warren to abandon Washington State the way he did.

CHAPTER 2

STICKING AROUND

DAD'S GONNA STAY

You would never imagine that the first thing you had to do, upon getting your first head coaching job, is to apologize to your team. You would love, after coaching for 15 or 16 years, to fill your first team meeting with nothing but positive things. My first team meeting as head coach at Washington State had far more negativism than any coach would ever want.

What could I tell them… how wonderful things were going to be? That I was here for the long haul? They'd heard all that. For them, it was like having a fourth father in four years. It's like going up to them and saying: "Your mom's been dumped again, and I'm the new man in the house." They'd heard the Jackie Sherrill spiel and the Warren Powers spiel, and here I come waltzing in. I just knew they couldn't make it through another one of those meetings. I knew they wouldn't believe me. They'd been betrayed too many times.

All I could say was, "Gentlemen, there is not one single thing I could tell you now that you'd believe. So it's up to me to prove to you that I'm not going to lie to you like the last two coaches have." I told them my rules, what I was all about, what I was going to demand from them, and that I intended to stick around, whether they believed me or not.

I'll tell you, the team meeting to start my second season went a whole lot better. I think they were shocked... hey, this guy is still here.

FIRST PRESS CONFERENCE

Washington State people had been through a lot. There had been some serious betrayals of trust. They were justifiably bruised and skeptical. At my first press conference, I made it as simple as I could. On a sheet of poster board, I wrote a message.

"First Answer: I Plan To Fulfill My Contract!"

I thought, hey, let's just get this out of the way up front. A roomful of media pretty much keeled over laughing. But it was as truthful and honest and convincing as I could be. And I'll tell you what, it cut through a lot of the conversation.

BIG MONEY

The cost of living isn't going to gobble you up in Pullman. That was a good thing for coaches in those days before the big contracts. When I arrived as a top assistant in 1977, my salary was a whopping $20,000. The next year, for my first head coaching position, the pay bump barely put me in a different tax bracket, at $32,000. That was it. No television contract. No media packages. No shoe deals. Thirty-two flat.

I could live with that; I had the job I wanted and could get by easily in Pullman. What worried me, though, was the status of my assistants, the highest paid of which was earning a skimpy $16,500, and some of them had to scrape by at $11,000 a year. Remember, this was not the Dark Ages, this was the late 1970s and early '80s.

So, I tried to help them out the best I could. We had a two-week football camp for kids and I took my slice of that and divvied it up between the assistants as a little bonus. One year athletic director Sam Jankovich offered me a $5,000 raise. I said I'd take it, but I'd split it up between my coaches as a little financial boost for them.

Twenty or so years later, Mike Price was pulling down $970,000 a year from the same school. From $32,000 to $970,000... that's more than keeping up with inflation, especially given the economy in the Greater Pullman Metropolitan Area. Mike got two teams to the Rose Bowl, for which I am extremely happy as a Cougar. But, man, that's a pretty big change.

I had my chances to cash in a couple times. Over the years, Arizona State, Wisconsin, Wyoming and Louisiana State offered opportunities. I was flat out told I could have the Arizona State job the year John Cooper took it. These jobs paid considerably more than I was making at WSU. Much, much more, in fact.

Don't get me wrong, money is about the biggest thing we need. People say it's not everything, but, man, it's at least tied for first place because it allows you to do the things you want to do. But I had told those people at WSU that I wasn't going to cut and run at the first success we had. I was committed to the place. My objective was to stay there long enough to put an end to all the jokes about coaching turnover. We did. And that was a pretty good reward in itself.

NOT SO FUNNY, PAL

In 1978, I became the fourth head football coach at Washington State in four years. It didn't take long before I had heard all the jokes I could stomach about the revolving door and the special Atlas Van Lines discounts. From the start, I wasn't going to stand for it, even if I had to rear back and get a little tough on occasion to make it stop. I was going to take none of it... not from a state legislator, not from anybody. Nobody was going to make fun of us in front of me. The problem was that not only did we have to fight off the California schools and the Arizona schools, but we had half the state laughing at us, too. We could not tolerate that. We had to change that image.

We could see the problem when we went into schools to recruit kids. Coaches would trot out players who weren't getting recruited by, say, Oregon and Washington. We had to tell them, no, wait a minute, if we can't beat Oregon and Washington with that second guy, that's not going to do us any good. Those are the people we're going to have to beat. They were in the habit of looking at us as second-class citizens and we couldn't put up with that.

Because we finally had some stability, with a great group of coaches for the next nine years, we were able to send the same

*No, it's not an ad for Brylcreem. The sideburns, pompadour,
and eager expression are all things I brought with
me to Washington State in the late 1970s.
(Photo courtesy of Washington State University)*

guys back into those schools where they developed the reputation for being first-rate people. The other thing that happened
was that the players we got learned that they could come to
Washington State and be coached with a certain amount of fun
and respect. And once players find they like it, they go home
to their coaches and friends saying how good it is. They start
selling the program for us.

Yes, I confronted a few people along the way. I remember
having to jump some emcees on the banquet circuit several
times. I would go to those things to sell the program; I always
figured that if they had a good image of Jim Walden, that
would present a good image of Washington State. At least half
a dozen times in those early years, the emcee would start off
with some jokes making fun of Washington State. Without
holding back, I took those guys apart. I'd say something like,
"I'm honored to be here, and Mr. Emcee, in listening to you
tonight, you have proven to me that, in some individuals, the
tongue is not always attached to the brain." I'd say it in a nice
way, but everybody got the message: I didn't come there to listen to people make fun of my school. It was an important first
step.

WALDENISM

When you're the fourth head coach in four years and
haven't had a lot of success, they can get after you pretty hard.
The one jab that I used to hear was pretty clever: They said our
scoreboard used to read "Home" on one side and "Winners"
on the other.

SAD BEGINNING

Tragedy hit our Cougar family only three days into my first fall camp as head coach. Hayward Harris, a big and lovable junior defensive tackle out of Tacoma, collapsed and died on the field. Everybody knew him as "Spud."

He had to clear up some eligibility issues, so he didn't practice the first two days of fall camp. He came out for his first practice in the night session of the third day. They were dressed in shorts and helmets, and it wasn't going to be a tough workout. In fact, they had done nothing but warm up and stretch before getting started with agility drills.

Spud was doing a little reaction drill, and when he walked to the end of the line, he just collapsed. He was dead when he hit the ground. There had been no contact, no exertion… goodness, he hadn't even broken a sweat. All of a sudden, the trainers were giving him mouth-to-mouth and pounding on his chest. He never regained consciousness.

It was so hard for these kids, facing the torment of seeing a teammate go down. There was no earthly way something like this should happen. Had it been an accident, maybe they could have gotten a handle on it. But to collapse and die on a football field like that was such a sad and tragic mystery to all of us. The autopsy never indicated the cause.

Spud was a joyful, wonderful big man with a huge smile. He was greatly loved and enormously missed.

MIKE WILSON

Sometimes coaches use the first play of a game to establish a tone. On the first play of the first game of the 1978 season, against UNLV, we had Jack Thompson open up with a deep ball to our young, sophomore receiver, Mike Wilson. Mike got open on a deep post; Jack hit him in stride, right on the money.

Mike dropped it. Flat out dropped it. At some point in that game, he dropped another one. You have to remember, at the time, Jack Thompson was the sacred cow, a Heisman Trophy candidate, and fans didn't like seeing anything going on that wasn't going to pump up Jack's stats and reputation. When Mike dropped two passes, he became a guy some fans almost never forgave. It's a shame because he's this big, good-looking receiver with a ton of talent. He had trouble shaking off the pressure that was created by that first game.

Unbeknownst to me, over the next four or five games, whenever a pass play was called that would make him the primary target, Mike would swap sides with Jimmy Whatley or whoever was over there so he had less chance of having the ball thrown his way. He just felt so bad, and it was so stressful for him that he wanted to avoid being in the position to drop more balls from Jack Thompson.

For a long while I'd hear fans grumbling about Mike Wilson. That was wrong, and I felt horrible about it. In the end, I'd have to say it made him one of the most underrated Cougars ever. He was almost obscure at Washington State, which was a shame because he was six foot three, had a 35-inch vertical leap, had great hands and was a terrific receiver. His 10 seasons in the NFL, and four Super Bowl rings with San Francisco, offer all the testimony you need on that matter.

APPLE CUP '78: LEARNING

The impact of this game on a head coach caught me totally off guard, as I was overwhelmed by the demands. I'd been involved in great rivalry games, Nebraska/Oklahoma and Miami/Florida battles. But not as a head coach. As it turns out, I had no idea what a difference that made.

I walked through the tunnel to our field for our Monday evening practice and I was stunned by the media there; cameras all over, and writers I'd never seen before. It kept up all week, with calls from papers in Bellevue and Everett to Vancouver and Wenatchee. It was very disruptive for me, and I spent time taking calls and doing media things when I needed to be working on game preparation. Honestly, I just was not ready for this.

We lost 38-8, and we just weren't very good. Even back then, I was wondering why we had to play our arch-rivalry game on a neutral field in Spokane. That didn't make sense. But they wore us out with their talent. I remember Michael Jackson being really a tremendous player, one of the first really fast linebackers who could run all over the place.

Jack Thompson had just broken the NCAA career passing record the week before at Arizona, but he was like the rest of us, having a day that we didn't want to remember. We committed nine turnovers, six of them interceptions of Jack's passes, as he was under heavy, heavy pressure all day. On the other side, Joe Steele killed us again, rushing for 196 yards.

It was terrible; we were grossly overmatched and maybe overwhelmed emotionally. But I looked at myself and figured I was a quick learner. And what came out of that for me was a firm understanding of how important that game was, and also the commitment that I would never again be unprepared. I promised that this was never going to be just another game for the Cougars.

I was brutally frank afterward, being quoted that of the 22 starters on the field, we didn't have more than four or five who could start for them. I don't think I got any criticism about that statement, because most people saw it was the truth. But I promised that was going to change starting that very minute.

CHAPTER 3

SELLING WASHINGTON STATE

WHEAT FIELDS VS. INTERSTATES

We coaches love to see ourselves as builders of character and shapers of young men. In the best cases, that's true. Of course, an awful lot of our job involves being salesmen. Every coach tries to emphasize the positives of his school and minimize the negatives. Face it, not everybody can appreciate the scenic wonders of the Palouse when they are first exposed to them. So, we learned ways to turn it around in our favor. Hey, agriculture can be beautiful.

From some recruits, we'd hear: "Why would I want to go to Washington State when it's right in the middle of a wheat field?" Our answer to that was: Why would you want to go anywhere that was right in the middle of an Interstate Highway system? Would you rather drive through pleasant wheat fields or see nothing but the butt-end of the automobile stuck in traffic in front of you? The schools we recruited against in the conference, Arizona State, the L.A. schools, the two schools in northern California, and Washington would attack us for being out in the fields. Yeah, well, some of us would rather look at tranquil fields of wheat than a bunch of wrecked cars along the freeway in Oakland.

The next thing recruits would ask was: "What is there to do up there?"

We'd turn that around, "Well, what is it you've been doing where you are?"

"Oh, we've got the Lakers in L.A."

"Fine, how many Lakers games have you been to?"

"None."

"Well, you can go to exactly the same number of Lakers games in Pullman. If you haven't been to one of those things, what's the difference if all of a sudden you ain't got 'em?"

I couldn't believe a young person thinking there was nothing to do in Pullman. I'd tell them, "Look, there's approximately 16,000 students with an average age of 20. Most of them are from a long distance away. There's probably 14,000 students on campus every weekend. Do the math. It doesn't take much imagination to figure out that being in an environment with that many people of your own age is going to create entertainment possibilities."

The one thing we could assure them was this: When you do find something to do, it's not going to cost you an arm and a leg.

NOT THE DATING GAME

Some schools get in needless trouble because they have forgotten one important fact: They run a football program, not an escort service. I know some places are very intent that football recruits have female companionship on their campus visits. But we never operated that way. I had come up through the Bob Devaney school of recruiting at Nebraska and we, as coaches, spent a lot of time with the recruit when they visited us.

Bob Devaney just didn't like the connotation of having girls as player escorts on campus. For one, what can a co-ed tell them about the program? A lot of these kids already have girlfriends at home, and it seemed like we would just be creating a problem.

That being said, it didn't take a genius to know that your player who is hosting him for the weekend is going to find whatever parties there are on campus that night. That happens everywhere. But it's a risky business, and that hasn't changed much over the years. Trouble can break out at a party any time, and a recruit can get caught right in the middle of it.

I can tell you that this is always a very nervous time for coaches. We just felt we didn't need the added worries about how somebody is treating a co-ed on top of it all. I'm sure some coaches these days who've found themselves in the middle of some nasty publicity are starting to share that opinion.

THE RECRUIT WAGON

As hard as we tried, we could never move Pullman any closer to the Spokane airport. Our recruits from Seattle would usually fly right into Pullman on those little tree-top planes, but most of the kids from elsewhere obviously had to fly into Spokane.

Without a doubt, to get off a plane and drive 80 miles through the wheat fields can be tough and pretty dull. I wouldn't argue that. So, we had to come up with a way to counteract it. Every year we rented a nice motor home about the first of November and kept it until February. We always tried to get as many guys as possible on the same flight so we could get 13 or 14 in that motor home and we could feed them sandwiches and hot chocolate and cookies.

We discovered that kids love to communicate with each other. Some of them may have played against one another, or were from different parts of California and wanted to exert bragging rights. They would get talking and eating and having fun and getting to know each other, and it turned out to develop bonds that reaped benefits for us far beyond the intended.

To be absolutely honest, we did it to keep them from looking out the window. But later, when kids were asked if they hated the drive from Spokane to Pullman, they'd say: "Nah, man, it went real quick." Well, heck, some of them never looked where they were. The first time they really saw the region was on their first trip back after they had signed with us. They'd be asking: "Hey, what's that stuff out there?"

It's wheat, man, it's wheat. Get used to it.

IT'S ALL DOWNHILL

A misperception we always worked against was that Pullman was somewhere near Alaska. That could be a hard sell to some of the kids from southern California who had never seen snow in their lives. We had to show them from the start that snow wouldn't kill them. In fact, it could be fun.

Washington State used to have its own ski hill, North-South Ski Bowl, across the state line over in Idaho. We checked it out with the NCAA and we found out we could legally take our recruits there to ski. The rule was that you couldn't pay for any activity that exceeded a certain allotted daily expense. Because we owned the place, the price was cheap enough that we could rig them up with skis and turn them loose on the mountain.

We'd load them into the motor home and take them over for night skiing. It was an eye-opening experience to see how well athletes could adapt to an activity they'd never tried. Two or three of our coaches, Lindsey Hughes in particular, were good skiers, so they showed them what to do. And it didn't take them but a time or two down the hill before they got pretty darn good at it. By the time we'd shut it down for the night, a lot of them were complaining that they didn't want to stop. Suddenly, all this snow and cold weather we had wasn't such a horrible thing after all.

It had such a positive impact that recruits would talk about it on other trips they were taking, and I bet we got turned in by every other school in the conference who thought we were spending too much on some fancy ski trip. But we checked it out a bunch of times and it was completely legal. All of a sudden, instead of hearing all that ah-it's-cold-up-there stuff, some of those kids would be like: "Yeah, so what, it's fun."

WSU-SPOKANE BRANCH

When we got started trying to figure out the best ways to recruit players to Washington State, we heard some intriguing stories about how previous coaches had "sold" the place, and had attempted to minimize the effect of Pullman's remote location. The story is told that one of them, Jim Erkenbeck, who was an assistant on Jim Sweeney's staff, was pretty creative.

According to a good source of mine, the first year that Erkenbeck came to WSU, he would fly recruits into Spokane. Okay, that's normal. But when they got there, he kept them in Spokane. Supposedly, he put them up at a nice hotel in town, took them out to Gonzaga and drove them around the campus, took them to Albi Stadium and then had a dinner at a fancy restaurant. As the story goes, some of them never made it to Pullman.

DRESSED FOR SUCCESS

I wouldn't ever cheat to get a recruit… but I'll admit I've committed a few moving violations on the way. Ricky Turner, a quick and elusive quarterback out of Compton, California, was high on our list of recruits one year because we needed an option quarterback who could also throw the ball. Ricky was only 178 pounds, but he had a Doug Flutie mentality, although he could run even better than Flutie.

Ricky was a highly coveted athlete… but not as a quarterback. Arizona State was in on him hard to be a wide receiver or defensive back. But we saw his potential as a game-breaker with the ball in his hands. We may have been the only school willing to give him the chance to play quarterback. As the recruitment got down to the wire, I was in Seattle for the annual Gold Helmet Award banquet. It was a predominately Washington event (Gold Helmet, duh), but I always went

*Ricky Turner couldn't help us much at USC in this 1981
loss, but landing him as a recruit met our needs for a great
running quarterback to operate our option offense.
(Photo courtesy of Washington State University)*

because they were kind enough to invite me to be a part of it. I headed off to this event in my tuxedo when I got a call from assistant Bob Padilla, who was recruiting Ricky.

"If you can get down here tonight and talk to Ricky and his grandmother, and look in their eyes and promise he'll play quarterback, I think we can sign him," Padilla told me. Ricky's grandmother had done a wonderful job reminding Ricky that his life-long dream had been to be a Division I quarterback. WSU, she told him, was a place that would allow that to come true. They just wanted assurances from the head coach.

I was never so anxious to see a banquet get over. I was so excited, I didn't change, I didn't pack, I raced to the airport in my tuxedo. I was speeding up one-way streets, going the wrong way, trying to get to the Seattle airport. I finally got on the red-eye flight to L.A., and man, I was the best-dressed guy on the Midnight Special. I got to Ricky's house at 8 the next morning, dressed like a maitre d', and he committed to us, no doubt impressed by our promises... and my wardrobe.

Our judgment of him as a quarterback was dead-on solid; he turned into a fabulous option quarterback with a powerful arm, who led us to a number of important victories between 1980 and 1983. We made a promise to his grandmother and we kept it. Plus, I'm sure I was the only head coach to show up at their house in formal wear.

TRAGEDY AVERTED...
GET ME TO THE AIRPORT

Recruiting is not a life-and-death matter... unless you had to spend much time on Washington Highway 195. Wade Killian, a linebacker prospect out of Everett, can offer testimony. At the very least, he could never say he didn't get an exciting recruiting trip from Washington State. Fortunately, a potential catastrophe turned into just a good story for all of us to tell.

Because we were shuttling cars and I was heading out on the road, two graduate assistants and I drove Wade back to the Spokane Airport after his recruiting visit. It was winter and that highway was treacherous. Scott Ricardo was driving, but he was from California and didn't know much about handling icy conditions. About 15 miles out of Spokane, we hit a patch of black ice. And if we weren't going sideways, at the very least the left rear wheel was gaining on the right front.

I told everybody to brace up because it didn't look good, and Scott hit the brakes… exactly the wrong thing to do. That Mercury started spinning off toward a bluff. There's really only a few places on that whole drive where there's much of a drop-off, and, of course, we couldn't have done this someplace where we could have just skidded off into a wheat field. We took off flying down that hill, and I don't even know how many times that Merc flipped. But it finally landed on its wheels and the roof was flatter than a fritter.

None of us was hurt, but I hit my knee on that dashboard so hard that it left a smudge of blue paint embedded in my gray dress slacks that I never could get out. Once we made sure everybody was all right, we kicked out one of the doors to squeeze out. Immediately, I was worried about the recruit. But he was okay. And Scott, he was worried that he almost killed the head coach.

We were maybe 15 feet down this gully in about four feet of snow. A guy drove up and I asked him if we could borrow a crowbar or a tire tool to force the trunk open to get our stuff out. And when he offered more help, I asked him to take the other three to the hospital to get them checked out.

Another car came up and the guy asked, "Hey, aren't you Coach Walden?" I confessed. When he asked if he could help in any way, I told him he could really help by taking me to the airport because I had a flight to catch to get to the four home visits in Los Angeles I had scheduled that night. Here's how deeply the importance of recruiting is ingrained in college coaches. We'd flipped the car down a bluff, we'd crawled up out of the snow, and my two concerns were getting the recruit to the hospital and getting me to the airport so I didn't miss any home visits.

The key question, of course: Did you get the kid? Darn right. Wade came and played for us and was a great contributor. I later asked him why in the world, after what happened, did he decide to come with us?

He said, "Coach, I just figured if we can get through all that together, we can make it through anything."

WE HAD HIM AT HELLO

Mark Rypien likes to kid me that I was so frantic making my recruiting spiel to him that he had to listen to me for an hour and a half before he could squeeze in his commitment to Washington State. I was in great form, giving him every speech I could think of: Stay home, love your parents, blah, blah, blah. I was so excited about giving a winning performance that I never slowed up enough to give him a chance to tell me he had already decided he was coming.

"Coach," he said patiently, "I already knew I wanted to go to Washington State."

What a moment that was for me and for WSU. Without a doubt, that agreement, made in the living room of the Rypien's

Spokane home, was the most important recruitment we ever had. He was our single biggest name. He could have gone anywhere; he could have called any Division I school in America and gotten interest.

Rypien had been a prep All-American at Shadle Park. He was big and strong and a marvelous athlete in basketball and baseball as well as football. The importance of wooing him was compounded by the fact that he was from Spokane, our backyard. I also knew how badly Washington wanted him.

His commitment gave us so much credibility, and put a stamp of legitimacy on our program. He was the best quarterback in the West, and his signing told people that there must be something pretty good going on in Pullman. I'll never stop appreciating that.

WALDENISM

You know those lists they have of the top 100 recruits? We found that once a guy committed to us, he'd drop about 45 places. They figured the guy can't be as good as they thought or he'd have gone somewhere else.

DEAD (MEAT) PERIOD

We always worked diligently to follow the rules. So, I almost jumped out of my skin the day a recruit showed up at my office door right in the middle of a dead period. As everybody but former Washington coach Rick Neuheisel knows, dead periods are times when the NCAA allows no contact between a recruit and a coach.

We had a defensive lineman named Keith London we were recruiting out of Glendale Junior College. Del Wight was recruiting him for us, and one of our former assistants, Bob Padilla, was on him for Arizona State. As it got close to signing day, this kid disappeared and both Del and Bob thought the other one had done something to stash him away.

But don't look now, this kid walks into my office, when he's not supposed to be anywhere near us, and I was immediately in total violation. Turns out, he met a girl on his recruiting trip and, on his own nickel, bought a plane ticket to Pullman with the intent of hanging out with her. He thought that since we didn't pay for the ticket, everything was fine. I told him it didn't matter, that he had to get out in a hurry.

He then unloaded another surprise. "I don't have the money to go home, I just want to hang out here until the semester starts," he said. He ended up getting a job over the weekend to buy a ticket home, and I called the NCAA to tell them what happened. They said it was fine, that I'd done all I could and had gone by the book. But I was nervous as heck. I told them, come on, you can't disbelieve a story like that.

He later showed up for fall camp and it didn't take long before we had to remove him from the team for disciplinary reasons. The funny thing was that I kept seeing this U-Haul truck in the lot across the street from Bohler Gym. Never moved. About the middle of September I asked the guys on the team if they knew anything about it. They said London had driven it up. A couple days after that, the city police came by my office trying to trace a stolen U-Haul truck.

RICKY REYNOLDS

You do your best to do your homework and eliminate the variables, but coaching and recruiting are inexact sciences. The way we lucked our way onto Ricky Reynolds is the perfect example. This guy was a spectacular cornerback, who went on to play 10 years in the National Football League, and we signed him with one phone call just a few days before fall camp opened.

They used to have a big coaches clinic associated with an All-Star game in the San Joaquin Valley of California. I was invited to be a speaker and I got to the hotel Friday evening, checked in, and headed down to the hotel bar to see if any other coaches were down there. When I sat down, a junior-college coach I knew came over and started shooting the bull. He asked me if anybody had ever told me about a kid named Ricky Reynolds out of Luther Burbank High in Sacramento. Well, no, I'd never heard of him.

Ricky had been injured his senior year and only played a few games as a running back and defensive back. But this coach claimed that Ricky was one of the best athletes in the valley and he was too good to be going to his jaycee. This kid, he said, is a four-year talent and he's scholastically eligible to play. The coach went further, adding that he'd stake his career on this kid. Now, that got my attention.

About an hour later, assistant coach Jimmy Burrow came in after watching the All-Star game and pulled me aside like he had this big secret. "I've got to talk to you," he said. "I just saw a player at this game who is really good, who hasn't signed with anybody, but Oregon thinks they're going to get him."

I said: "Is his name Ricky Reynolds?" Jimmy's eyes got really big and he looked at me like I was a fortune teller. Jimmy had his number and said he thought all we had to do was call him at 11 and we could make our pitch. Ricky was so excited he could barely get his breath, and we offered him a scholarship on this coach's advice and Jimmy seeing him play in that one game.

The funny part of it is that Oregon coach Rich Brooks waited to call him on Saturday morning, and Ricky had to tell him that he already had committed to us.

Now, here's a kid who started at corner for us for three seasons, had a fabulous NFL career, and we got him as a one-call recruit less than a week before he had to show up in Pullman. Sometimes you get lucky. Sometimes you bump into the right guy in a bar.

WALDENISM

People confuse negative recruiting with cheating. Hell-fire, those are way different. If you go into a car dealer, the Ford guy is going to tell you how much better his rig is than a Chevy; that's business. Apply that to coaching, and you know somebody is going to say, "Our weight room is better than theirs." I think you've got a right to tell them what you've got. If you're going against Joe Paterno, who's 77, or Bobby Bowden, who's 101, other teams are naturally going to mention that those guys might not be around your whole time. The thing about "negative" recruiting is that it doesn't look like it works very well.

CHAPTER 4

COMING HOME

PULLMAN, SWEET PULLMAN

Some people had the mistaken notion that I had a problem with Spokane. I didn't dislike Spokane at all; I simply despised Albi Stadium, and the nonsensical concept of having to play our home games 80 miles from our campus. Younger fans don't even remember this, but when I took over the WSU program, we played most of our important games at Albi Stadium.

UCLA wouldn't play us in Pullman, only at Albi. Washington wouldn't play us in Pullman, only at Albi. USC somehow got away from playing us just about anywhere in the state of Washington. It was that way for something like 30 years. For all those years in the Pac-8 Conference, three of WSU's seven opponents wouldn't come to our campus. How could any team be competitive under those circumstances?

Early on, I had about all I could take of that situation. I felt it was an injustice to our students, having to drive to

Spokane, and never being able to just walk across campus to watch a game against UCLA or Washington. On top of that, Albi was basically a high-school stadium. You'd go into the locker rooms and you had to hang your clothes on nails. You had to spend the day busing up there, and it made us feel like we were always on the road. There was not one good thing about Albi if you were the coach at WSU.

I went in to see Dr. Glenn Terrell, WSU president, who had a great influence on me, and was one of the greatest friends a football coach could ever have. We were talking about salary raises, and I told him there was something I wanted more than money. I wanted him to promise me he'd make an effort to get us out of Spokane. As was his way, he patiently said, "Jim, give me your reasons."

I went through them for about two hours. I applied it to the students, facing the problems of the road to Spokane, and the potential drinking; it wasn't safe. It wasn't on our campus, and was inconvenient for the team and the fans.

And then I applied it to the state legislators. I asked him: How long has it been since those people who control the funding for this university have even set foot on this campus? How can we sell the value of this university to them when all they ever do is come to Spokane, spend the night at the Ridpath Hotel, take in the game, and drive back to Seattle without ever coming to Pullman? That hit a nerve with him; he really seemed to grasp that.

The next thing I knew, we were announcing that we were starting a project to dig out our stadium to expand it to 37,000 or 38,000, which would force the other schools to come to Pullman to play us. I know athletic director Sam Jankovich took some heat from people who asked why we needed to do that since we rarely filled the stadium as it was. But he did a great job getting that done, and it was clearly one of the most positive things to happen to Washington State football.

I'm certain this program never could have gotten where it is now without that move back to campus. I know it was crucial in three of the biggest wins we had while I was at WSU, the 1979 upset of UCLA on the day we dedicated the new stadium, the 1982 upset of the Washington Huskies in their first trip to the Palouse in 28 years, as well as our first victory in three decades over USC when they finally came to campus in 1986.

THANK YOU, COME AGAIN

For Washington State, no games can ever rival the importance of the Apple Cup. But the first real stamp of legitimacy for our program came on October 13, 1979, with an enormous win over UCLA. In this case, the location was almost as relevant as the outcome. In fact, I'm certain it played a role in the outcome.

Because of their power in the conference and their ability to force us into scheduling games against them in Spokane, UCLA had not visited us in Pullman since 1955. But when Martin Stadium was enlarged, we were able to leverage them into a Palouse visit… and that change of venue paid enormous dividends. When we started thinking about which game to select for the stadium dedication ceremonies, the UCLA game was a natural, and it was also designated as Homecoming that year.

We were coming off three straight losses and UCLA had a great football team, with one of the best I-backs in the country in Freeman McNeil. We won, 17-14. I'm sure coaches who came later to WSU have no idea how huge that was just to get

*The expansion of Martin Stadium allowed us to stop the
ridiculous charade of playing "home games" in Spokane.
We finally got a chance in 1979 to start teaching the
USCs and UCLAs the joys of visiting Pullman.
(Photo courtesy of Washington State University)*

teams like that on our home turf. I never cared if Martin
Stadium was big enough to bring in big intersectional games
against Ohio State or Tennessee. But I did care about winning
the conference, and you can't win the conference if you're playing all the toughest opponents either on the road or at a neutral site.

To beat them at home gave us so much credibility, and it
surely added to our level of competitiveness against those top
teams.

MARTIN STADIUM

One of the reasons Martin Stadium felt so cozy for us, and so awful for visitors, was because the stands are right down on top of the benches. It was so close that the guys in the front-row seats could hear your speeches to the players. I was over there chewing out a defensive linemen one game and some guy from the front row leaned over and said, "Yeah, give 'em hell, coach."

SEEING ORANGE

Of the great opposing players we faced, few dominated us like Art Monk in late September of 1979. We played Monk's Syracuse Orangemen in Buffalo in front of only 10,000 fans. Monk would go on to be one of the greatest receivers in National Football League history, and I can only assume that we helped build his confidence along the way.

The story of the Art Monk game, though, is about another player... Paul Kalina, a little walk-on cornerback out of Selah, Washington. Paul looked like former Cougar baseball player Ron Cey: He walked like a duck and he looked like a duck. Only he didn't quack. Paul was maybe five foot nine and may have run a 4.9 in the 40-yard dash. He was only a second-year freshman, I think, so he wasn't just small and slow, he was green as a gourd, on top of it.

We had a couple injuries at cornerback and, don't look now, but all we had left to guard Art Monk was Paul Kalina. Bless his heart, he did his best, but we simply could not line up

Aside from those aluminum bleachers that made a great racket when our fans kicked them, the best part of Martin Stadium was how close the fans were to the sidelines. Students never felt bashful about shouting out coaching tips to me. (Photo courtesy of Washington State University)

Paul deep enough that Art Monk couldn't run past him. It was one of the greatest mismatches ever. Art Monk just wore us out, and there was not a single thing we could do about it. We got beat 52-25, and the only good thing about it was there was nobody in the stands and the game wasn't on television.

SAMOA SAMOA

I don't know that I ever coached anybody who had a more pure and joyful love of the game than Samoa Samoa. He was addicted to football, almost compulsive about it. He wanted to play every down, and I had a hard time just getting him to come off the field. He begged me to give him a chance to return kickoffs. He pleaded to be on punt-coverage teams. If he had his way, he would have played quarterback, tight end, linebacker and free safety. He might have been able to, too.

It wasn't just in the games, either, he loved to practice. He'd always be on the field before anybody else and sometimes he'd drag a manager out there to throw the ball with him. He brought such a sense of competitiveness and joy to be out there that it was contagious, and it made him a great leader. He also may have been about the best athlete we ever had at quarterback. We got him out of junior college and he came in Jack Thompson's last year, so we only got one good year out of him. That was a shame because all of us really enjoyed being on the field with him. He just could never get enough of the game of football, and it's so wonderful to teach such an eager pupil.

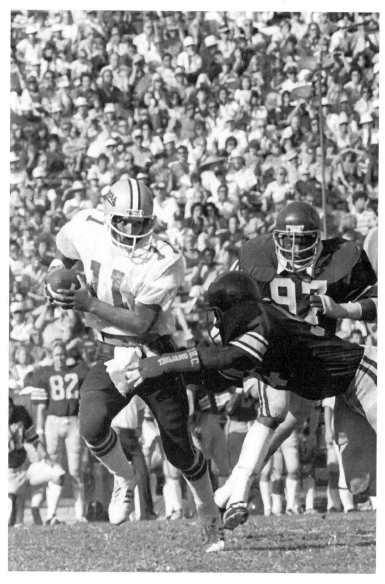

Samoa Samoa could not only do everything, he actually wanted to give every position a try. Here he's trying to dodge USC tacklers. Even facing off against the powerful Trojans was a joy for Samoa. (Photo courtesy of Washington State University)

APPLE CUP '79: MOTIVATION

We learned some things from that '78 Apple Cup, mostly just how far we had to step it up to be competitive. The '79 game with Washington was the first time I really challenged guys to understand their roles in this, to grasp the importance of this rivalry game. That part of it was our responsibility. Washington had won five in a row and our guys had to know that it was up to us to make this a rivalry. Look, gentlemen, this is no rivalry if we don't supply some competition.

I could tell they had received the message, and we went over there feeling much stronger. It was a time for us to really show them that there's a new Cougar in the state and we weren't going to allow ourselves to be an afterthought anymore. That was at a time when some people were saying that Washington State didn't need to be in the Pac-10 Conference, and I'm not so sure some Washington people weren't pouring fuel on that fire. We needed to make a statement. And I think we did.

We had come off a 38-8 thumping the year before in Spokane, and they had most of their guys back and were about to finish 10-2. But we played our butts off, especially Steve Grant at quarterback, and I was so proud of our guys. We lost 17-7, but that was a great Husky team. They scored twice late in the second quarter, including a nice post-corner route from Tom Flick to Paul Skansi right before halftime.

It was another game under heavy rain, but it showed me that we were regrouping as a team, and learning how to coach as a staff. We were getting better at evaluating, and more importantly, we learned how much emotion we needed to bring into that game every year.

JOB INSECURITY

When I took the job in 1978, there was a lot of hubbub about all the turnover we'd had. I was, after all, the fourth head coach in four years. Because I was so committed to sticking around for a while and putting an end to the instability, it came as a real shock when I started hearing rumors in the 1980 season that athletic director Sam Jankovich was thinking about firing me. We weren't having the greatest of seasons (we finished 4-7), but I had taken over a monstrosity and was just two and a half seasons into trying to build the foundation of something that would last.

I started hearing that Sam was seeking counsel from boosters around the state and testing the water for support if he decided to go ahead with the firing. I know for a fact this went on, because trusted sources told me as much. I have to tell you, I was quite offended that he was ready to fire me after having made such a big to-do about all the coaches that had left him prematurely. Actually, it went beyond my being offended; I was awfully mad.

Spokane *Chronicle* columnist Charlie Van Sickel told me that Sam had approached him to try to gauge what his editorial response would be if he fired me. Charlie told me that he was very clear in his message that he would make Sam's life miserable every day if he fired me because he thought I had the program going in the right direction. I was very humble about that strong support.

Sam went all the way to President Terrell, Glenn later told me. President Terrell said he told Sam that he always supported his deans and their decisions. But he was so certain it was the wrong thing to do, that if Sam fired me, he'd expect Sam's resignation within the next several days. Thankfully, for me, it didn't get done. And the next year we had the Cougars in their first bowl in half a century. Along the way, we had to overcome a lot of negatives and had to convince people that the program was on sound footing. It was nice to know there were enough people out there who liked what we were doing.

Sam did a great deal for us at WSU, but I think in this case he was a young AD and a little impetuous and he wanted results immediately. We get along, but something like that doesn't exactly make you bosom buddies for life. It all worked out in the end, but it's an example of the impermanence of coaching that people don't always hear about.

ALLAN KENNEDY

Rarely can you point to one guy as the primary influence on the rest of the team in any specific regard. But tackle Allan Kennedy truly stood as the motivator for Cougars at the time, and probably afterward, for pure devotion in the weight room. He was the first really massive linemen I'd seen. We had always liked those smaller guys who could get out and scramble into their blocks. But Allan was unbelievably huge, six foot seven, 275 pounds, and I mean sculpted. I'll give him credit for setting a pattern with his passion for weight training. His attitude cultivated an expectation among young players regarding the importance of working out. We made him captain of the weight room and he was the best influence some of these kids could have had.

Keith Millard, in particular, just loved Al Kennedy. Kennedy was his hero, and he'd get up early Saturday mornings just so he could go be in the weight room with Big Al.

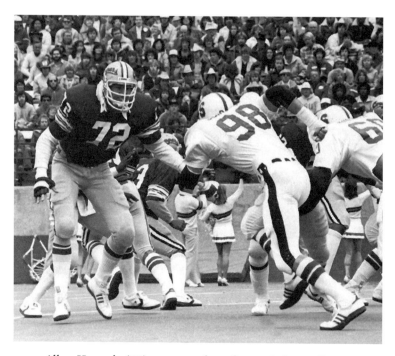

Allan Kennedy (72) was one of our first truly huge offensive linemen. He never had much to say, but he was one of the all-time greats who established a work ethic in the Cougar weight room that was legendary. (Photo courtesy of Washington State University)

Kennedy was so quiet, though. He never said anything. He'd block his man, walk back to the huddle, and then he'd come back and block him again. No discussion. He didn't have to say much; all his teammates had to do was watch him in the weight room and watch him on the field. He had a terrific positive impact on our team for years.

MUST BE TATE'S FATE

Running back Gary Tate rarely played, but every season was a banner year for him.

My policy was that players had to live on campus as freshmen and sophomores because I thought it was important they mix among the rest of the student body and socialize with the regular students. Gary Tate, in the late '70s, evidently assimilated so well that he quickly developed a loyal fan club among his friends in the dorm.

His first year, his whole dorm floor would sit together up in a corner at the scoreboard end of the stadium—maybe as many as 20 guys—and every game they held up this banner that read: "Gary Tate Will Be Great."

Gary wasn't playing much. He wasn't a bad player, but not great, and there were some guys ahead of him playing well. Every Monday, in our coaches' meetings, we'd get all over Gary Gagnon, our running backs coach, asking him why he wasn't playing Gary Tate. After all, we'd read that he's going to be great.

The next year came along and Gary still wasn't playing much. He was a tough kid and a great scout team player and a nice contributor. But he couldn't get on the field much. For the first game, there it was, the new banner: "We Can't Wait For Tate."

Come on, Coach Gagnon, you gotta play this guy, he's gonna be great, and his buddies can't wait. It got to be a lot of fun for us, and we had some anticipation what the sign would read the third year. Right before the season, though, Gary Tate decided he'd had enough football and quit the team. We were disappointed, but his dorm buddies hung in there with him and put up a final banner:

"It's Too Late For Tate."

APPLE CUP '80: IMPROVEMENT

We were gaining on 'em. This felt like the second time that our players really caught on to the importance of this game, and we lost 30-23 in Spokane, which was important because we had played so miserably there two years before.

They had some great players, as usual, but we were asking no quarter and giving none. That last half of the 1980 season, we had finished pretty strongly (3-3 over the last six weeks), and it seemed like the team was finally figuring out what was going on.

We got all over Husky quarterback Tom Flick early, intercepting him twice before he completed his first pass to a teammate. We pulled out 14-0. In a span of a minute and a half late in the first half, though, they scored twice to tie it at 14. Flick finished with three long touchdown passes, but we were still threatening until Husky safety Ken Gardner picked off Samoa Samoa with slightly more than a minute left in the game to help UW earn the Pac-10 title.

I told the press afterward that we hadn't gone up to Spokane with the goal of coming close, we came up there to win the game. But, in truth, I came out of that game feeling we had something special started. We had scored 23 points on them and lost by seven. We had scored just eight and seven against them the two previous Apple Cups, so to put up 23 showed there were some really positive things happening. Things were really looking up.

MY TOUGHEST COUG,
JIMMY WHATLEY

Jimmy Whatley, a 170-pound receiver out of Bellevue, refused to listen to me. He told me he was going to play in the Apple Cup game of 1980, and there wasn't much I could do to stop him. The tricky part about this was that he had broken his leg only three weeks before, and he was supposed to wear his cast for something like eight weeks. This was his senior year, he said, and there was absolutely no way he was going to miss his final game against Washington. All week, he told me and he told the doctors that he was going to cut the cast off before the game and come running out of that tunnel.

Sometimes players put things in such a way that you just know you're helpless to change their minds. He wasn't asking permission, he was telling me the way it was going to be. He did exactly as he threatened. He cut that cast off in the training room before the game. He was a little wobbly, but he stood next to me most of the game, and whenever there was a play that he didn't have to run a primary route or get too involved, he went in.

He was one of the fiercest blockers we ever had, even for being so small. He loved to come inside and crack on the linebackers. He knew he couldn't run routes and he'd be hurting the team if he tried. But he threw his body around in there blocking. It was one of the most courageous things I'd ever seen, and that effort, to me, exemplified how unbelievably important that game is to these kids.

WALDENISM

If there was a bad thing that could happen involving scheduling, you know they'd do it to us. In '77, we opened with four road games and it wasn't until the seventh game of the year that we had our second game in Pullman. In '85, we opened with three straight conference games. I know people think I was paranoid, but some of the things they did to us were absurd. When it came to being a whipping boy in the conference, Washington State was it. I used to have a rule, if they have a conference meeting, we better make dang sure not to miss it, because we're not gonna like what they do to us if we're not there to stick up for ourselves.

CHAPTER 5

LIFE IN PULLMAN

EDGING COSTS EXTRA

George Raveling, our charismatic basketball coach, lived three doors down from me in Pullman. It's a small town, so that's not so unusual. I used to drop by quite often when I needed to talk things over. He had a signal for me: He'd leave the bathroom light on if he was home, and that would let me know it was okay to drop in.

He was a little bit of a man of mystery in the summers, though. He was one of the first coaches to really organize extensive camps, and he was in town for those. But otherwise, who knew where he would go? He might be anywhere in the world.

My son Murray used to mow his lawn… he was George's lawn boy. But Murray also played American Legion baseball in the summers and that would keep him busy, too. One day we drove past George's house and the grass was well over ankle

high. I said, "Murray, you better get over there and do Coach
Raveling's yard or you're gonna need a hay cutter." The problem was, he had a baseball game that day.

That afternoon, I mowed my yard, which was always one
of my chores, and I thought, what the heck, I'll do George's
while I'm at it. I had forgotten that Charlie Van Sickel of the
Spokane *Chronicle* was going to come down that day to do a
preseason interview. First thing you know, Charlie rolled
around the corner and saw me jockeying the mower. He got
out of the car and then it hit him, "Hey, isn't this George's
lawn?" He made a big deal out of it, writing that if anybody
had any worries about race relations in Pullman, all they had
to do was see the white football coach who grew up in
Mississippi mowing the lawn of the black basketball coach.

George had a lot of fun with it, too. At Cougar Club gatherings, he'd love to say, "And now, I'm pleased to introduce my
yard man, Jim Walden."

I'M IN THE BOOK

Sometimes when the phone would ring in the middle of
the night, my wife Janice would just roll over and shake her
head at me. I know this isn't customary protocol for a head
coach, but I never had an unlisted phone number.

Granted, you come to learn that the phone can be your
worst enemy. For a football coach, if the phone rings after midnight, it's not good news. Nobody calls you after midnight
with news you want to hear. My first thought was always that
one of my players was in trouble. Keep in mind, when I was at
Washington State, I had three teenage kids… and also about

100 of somebody else's teenagers. So, I was always fretting over a "family" of about 100 kids.

But in 17 years with my number in the book, I got only one or two nasty calls, and none that I can remember being really bad or frightening. Even if there were some complaints, I felt it was part of my job to deal with them; after all, it's not like we had a staff ombudsman to handle these matters. What I got mostly, believe it or not, was drunks asking me to settle bar bets at 1 or 2 in the morning.

"Hey, coach, glad I caught you, this is so-and-so down at the Trade Winds."

Sure, what can I do for you?

"My buddy says that this-and-such happened and I say so-and-so happened… we got a pitcher ridin' on it. Who's right?"

You had to have a sense of humor to enjoy these calls, but some of them were pretty entertaining. Every now and then I'd get a call just checking to make sure it was me. "Hey, coach, just discovered your number was in the book, thought I'd try it out to see if it was really you."

Most of the time I'd talk to them for a while. That didn't hurt me, except for Janice giving me that look. There were some nights after bad games when I half expected to get crank calls, when I thought I probably deserved nasty calls. I had my speech ready. If they'd have laid into me, I'd have stopped them and said, "Hey, go no further, I agree with you totally… I don't know why you didn't call sooner."

The biggest reason I kept my number listed was fairly serious. I never wanted to have a situation where a parent of a player could not get in touch with me in case of an emergency. There were several times every year when somebody's grandmother passed away or somebody's close relative got in a car accident. With that many players on a team, family emergencies could be an almost everyday occurrence. There's nothing more worrisome to a parent than not being able to get hold of a child when they needed to.

I could handle the idea of a few crank calls, but I never would have been comfortable with the thought that a parent couldn't get through to one of the players when they needed to because I had an unlisted number.

JANICE'S HUSBAND

I've heard coaches tell horror stories of how their children suffered hazing and ridicule in schools after the team lost a game or ran into a stretch of bad play. Thankfully, that was never the case in Pullman. My kids didn't seem to suffer too much for their dad's coaching indiscretions. Pullman is a forgiving town. There were a lot of kids whose parents were employed at the university. And students at Pullman High weren't going to bother my kids much because dad coached a bad game.

We used to complain that there weren't enough places to eat in Pullman, but how many do you really need, anyway? The most important thing was that great small-town atmosphere for the kids. It was funny, in fact, that the friends of my kids would always be running through the house and they never saw me as anything else but Emily and Lisa and Murray's father.

I'd say, "Hey, don't you know I'm somebody important?" And they'd just laugh.

My wife used to sell real estate in town, so she knew everybody... knew more people than I did. Pullman was the kind of place where we'd walk down the street and a lot of the folks we'd come across would wonder, "Hey, who's that guy with Janice?"

DADDY'S BUSY, DEAR

A lot of times a coach can't be around his kids; and sometimes even when you're in the same place, you can't do much to help them. My daughter Lisa was on the Cougar yell squad one year when we went to Seattle for the Apple Cup. She and her friends had hooked up a big "Go Cougars" banner on the fence at one end of the field.

They were yelling and cheering before the game and John Pease, the Huskies' defensive line coach, evidently heard enough out of them because he went over and ripped down their banner. Lisa was indignant as heck and marched over to get my attention. She wanted me to do something about it… right now, in fact. I said, honey, I've got some other stuff going that I've got to attend to just about now.

Oh, she was hot. After the game, to calm her down, I told her that I'd call Don James and ask him if he could please keep his coaches from tearing down my daughter's signs. Of course I didn't, but at least it settled her down.

RULES OF ENGAGEMENT

People like to talk, even if there's nothing to talk about. So most coaches learn how important it is to maintain an air of propriety. That's especially true in a town as small as Pullman.

You know that some of your older kids are 21 and are going to have a beer on occasion in a public place. So, I had a policy, if I walked into a place and a player was there, the player had to leave. But my unofficial rule, that they came to understand, was that I would try to stay away from places they might be. Sometimes I would give out hints where the coaches might be going, so we could stay off each others' territory.

If you were 21 and having a beer with your family or your girl in a restaurant, finish the beer and don't have another one while I'm there. I don't want you jumping up and running out of there like the place is on fire, but finish up. If you didn't do that, you'd have people all over town making up stuff about Walden being in the bar drinking with his players. People love to do that, and it's the kind of thing that can give a program a bad image if you're not careful.

WALDENISM

I hated a bunch of rules. It's too complicated for the kids. I didn't have many: Be on time and look decent. If you got in trouble, we dealt with it as it came up. The problem is, you are always outnumbered. I didn't feel like I had enough imagination to come up with a rule against every kind of trouble a player could possibly get into.

RUSTY'S TAVERN

Rusty's Tavern should be named a National Historic Place. They should erect a statue of Rusty Winters in that town. Rusty has passed away, but he was a legend. The rite of passage for every Washington State student was to turn 21 and go down to Rusty's and have a beer. If you put out a call for a reunion of Rusty's bartenders, it would be magnificent the people who would show up.

Rusty was such a character; he didn't have a car, and he'd just walk the block from his house to the bar and to the bank and back. As far as I know, that's all he ever did. One time we took him for a ride and he was shocked to see that stuff was built up down on the north end of town. He'd never been down the street that far.

As coaches, we never went in there during the year, because you've got to give players their space. But we would go in during those hot Pullman summers and shoot the bull. Rusty was not exactly a stickler for cleanliness, but he had the place painted one time, and for a couple years after that, his air condition never worked. It really got steamy in there during those hot stretches we'd get.

I finally told him, Rusty, you've got to get that air conditioner fixed 'cause, man, it's unbearable in here. He said he didn't think it was worth it. Well, if you don't care about it, then you won't mind if I climb up there and give the thing a whack or something to see if we can get some air movin' in here. This thing was like 15 feet in the air, so I got a ladder and crawled up there and couldn't believe what I saw. The thing was unplugged; it had been sitting there through two miserably hot summers without being plugged in. I plugged it in and the dang thing started humming like crazy.

He was such a funny guy. He'd take pictures of people and put them up in there like it was a Hall of Fame. It was an honor because he was real choosy about it. If you moved or did something he didn't like, he'd turn your picture around to face the wall. He had a million stories, too. I'm really sorry that somebody never sat down with him to write all the stories he had, because he was such a character and he never forgot a thing.

All the students related to that guy, and his passing truly left a hole in Pullman. He just wasn't very good with air conditioners.

SUMMIT MEETINGS

Very few people knew this, but the two head football coaches in Pullman used to meet every Monday afternoon from 4:30 to 6. Every Monday for nine years, Pullman High coach Ray Hobbs would come down to my office and we would talk. Ray was such a wonderful individual, who meant so much to football in the region. I just loved him, and I loved him for what he did for my son, Murray. Murray was just a little-bitty guy with a big heart, and he learned a lot under Ray Hobbs during times when I was busy coaching my own football teams.

Sometimes when we'd get together, we'd look at Ray's scouting report and he'd ask my opinion on, say, what the Medical Lake High offense was doing. If this guy goes this way, would you send that guy that way? That sort of thing. Some of it was blackboard stuff and getting my opinion. It was almost always something he knew already, but it was fun to bounce ideas off each other.

I don't know how many college coaches have weekly sessions with the local high school coach, but I know I enjoyed it. It was just two guys taking time to talk about football and life.

PEN PAL

At one point, I started getting letters fairly regularly from a guy who, it appeared, was in some sort of an institution or incarceration. He would have a note on the inside telling me how much he loved the Cougars, but on the outside of the envelope, he would write all sorts of rants about different things.

I always tried to be nice to people, so I would write him back, thanking him for his interest and support. I kept it pretty generic, but I figured it wouldn't hurt me to take a moment to write back. Then he started writing that he hoped to come up and see us some time. I told him that he would enjoy attending a game and I hoped he would be able to do that.

Maybe a couple years later, I was out of town recruiting when one of my kids came home from school to find a guy sitting on our front steps. He asked if Coach Walden was home. No. Okay, how about Mrs. Walden? Janice was working, but when she got home, this guy announced: "I'm here." She hadn't a clue who he was, so she asked: "Here to do what?" He informed her that he had written to me and I had invited him up for a visit.

Well, you're in Pullman, and you don't expect anything bad there. And this guy seemed to have my okay, so she invited him in and they talked for a while before he announced he had to go. She said she'd give him a ride downtown, but he said he'd walk. She could tell something wasn't right. He stayed around until I got home. I went down and met him for a cup of coffee, and we visited for some time before he told me he had to catch a bus.

This all happened on a weekend. Monday morning I got a call from his care facility, or whatever it was. They said he wasn't dangerous, but he did have some problems. He'd gotten away, and he wasn't supposed to be running around. I'm just glad he was a Cougar fan, not a hostile Husky.

ASH SUNDAY

The sky to the west got so ominously dark, the reflected light made it seem as if the sun were setting in the east... at 2 o'clock on a Sunday afternoon. It was stunning how profoundly the eruption of Mount St. Helens, a couple hundred miles to the west, affected Pullman. That encroaching dark cloud dropped volcanic ash across the Palouse several inches deep. It was like nothing we'd ever been through.

It was a couple days before they even let anybody get out of their houses except for emergencies, and school was closed. It was right in the middle of spring ball for us, and by the time we got out to look at the field, it was covered in so much ash it looked like somebody had dropped a million tons of cement dust on it. We went down and got 50 or 60 snow scoops and had the team out there shoveling. We spent probably two days trying to clear the field.

Bless their hearts, the players not only cleared the field, they did a lot of volunteering in the community, too, shoveling out cul-de-sacs and helping people clean off streets. There

No, this isn't a new offensive line drill. The eruption of Mount St. Helens in 1981 left several inches of volcanic ash on our football field. If we were going to finish spring practices, these guys had to get out the shovels and clear the way. (Photo courtesy of Washington State University)

was nothing much else to do, there was no school, but nobody could go home.

Some of the grocers in town told me that the strange natural disaster led to unexpected consequences. The distributor trucks couldn't deliver, and the students were out of school with nothing else to do. So, in about three days, there was not a single beer in any cooler in Pullman. Mount St. Helens' eruption, it turned out, left Pullman dry.

CHAPTER 6

COUGARS TAKE A HOLIDAY

REBUFFING COLORADO

By saving my butt in a game I coached horrendously, my team let me know early on that 1981 was going to turn into a special season. For the second game, at Colorado, I constructed the most awful offensive game plan ever devised in the history of college football. I screwed up the offense that game as badly as any coach ever did.

When you come out of games, you look at two things: Was the plan good and the play bad, or was the plan bad and the play good? Well, at Colorado, the plan was horrible. We thought we'd go in there and use an unbalanced line, and I mean to tell you it stunk to high heaven. But our defense played lights out and we were down only 10-0 with about four minutes left in the game.

I'll bet we hadn't made three first downs the entire game, and it was an embarrassment. We were running out of time, but we held them at about their 40. Coach Job Fabris asked: "We've got to take some chances, do you want to try to block this punt?" Why not, we've got to try something. Well, Jeff Keller, bless his heart, broke through, and sure enough blocked the punt. The thing took one hop and hit Paul Sorenson right in the chest. He ran something like 50 yards with it for a touchdown.

Okay, now we were only down 10-7 and we stopped them again near midfield. What the heck, let's try to block it again. Sure, enough, we broke through there and the punter saw he couldn't get it off, so he pulled it down and we tackled him.

We put Ricky Turner in at quarterback and he drove us lickety-split down to the 2-yard line with less than a minute to play. At that point, I realized we were going to have a great season. We planned to run an outside option, but Ricky inadvertently put the ball out and it hit off the hip of the lead back. But what could have been a disastrous fumble just bounced right back up to him and he ran around the end for a touchdown and we won 14-10.

I'll bet we didn't have 150 yards in offense the whole day, and our punt-return team won the game for us. I've never seen a dumber game plan. After that, I had to give the staff a hard time for it. I told them it was their fault for not stopping me from myself.

PAT BEACH

Pat Beach owes me a wad of money. He was one of our more likeable and pleasant guys who also was a real character. Pat was a talented tight end who had originally committed to the University of Puget Sound on the theory that he didn't

Pat Beach (89) celebrates a big play with receiver Paul Escalera.
Beach was actually uplifting for the entire team, as he was one
of the true characters who helped make Washington State a fun place
to play football. (Photo courtesy of Washington State University)

want to play Division I football. During the summer he changed his mind and decided he'd give us a try. We told him that we thought he'd make a terrific center, but we'd give him a chance to prove to us that he could be productive at tight end, which he did. The job he really wanted to get out of after a while was long-snapping. He was just so good at it, though, I convinced him to stay because that would turn out to be his ace in the hole. Long after he was worth a hoot as a tight end in the NFL, he could stay an extra two or three seasons just snapping the ball. I told him at the time that he was going to owe me a 10-percent cut of his salary for every year he stayed in the league just as a snapper. I think he went three extra years that way. I've never seen a check from him, though.

Pat had this unforgettable thing he would do before our Monday night practices, a habit that I missed dearly when he was gone. When he'd head out for special teams practices on Monday nights—and it would get darker and darker as the season went on—he would come through that tunnel and howl just like a wolf. I swear, it would send chills up your spine. If you closed your eyes you'd swear you were in the wilds of Montana. Granted, some of our players would howl at the moon in other ways, but Pat Beach was the only one who could unleash that chilling, mournful sound that let us know that Monday night's practice was about to start.

PAUL SORENSON

Paul Sorenson was simply flat-out dangerous. Not just to opponents, either. We used to kid him that he always went 100 miles an hour… but not always in the right direction. He may clobber an opposing receiver, or he may break the ribs of a fel-

This is a rare picture of Paul Sorenson not making contact.
It took Paul a while to figure out that you're only supposed to hit
the guys on the other team, but he was always a wrecking crew.
(Photo courtesy of Washington State University)

low Cougar defender. The only certainty was he was going to get near the ball and hit somebody.

He came in as a junior-college transfer and we loved his aggressiveness at free safety. He was so tough, but he was killing our guys, and we didn't have that many to go around. In our first three or four games in his first fall with us, he probably picked up five unnecessary roughness penalties for hitting guys out of bounds. His theory, I guess, was if he was going to run all the way from the middle of the field, he was going to be sure to get a lick in. Didn't matter if the guy was off the field and under the bench. Between hitting guys late and damaging his teammates, Paul started to become a detriment, and I had to call him on it.

I tried like the devil to get him to understand how to channel this aggressiveness for the forces of good. I told him if he got just one more penalty I was going to sit him and he wasn't going to get to play. I knew that would kill him. To his credit, he realized I was serious and he managed to stay aggressive but to be smarter about it. And he became a delight to coach.

When you hear people talk about a player having a reckless disregard for his body, that was Paul. I never could understand that; I always liked my body and I didn't want any parts of it broken. Paul simply did not seem to care. He threw it around like nobody you've ever seen. I will say that if he played in the defenses now, the way they use free safeties on blitzes, he'd have been an absolute terror, one of the best ever.

APPLE CUP '81: PAINFUL

We already knew we had eight wins and a bowl game to go to, which was a breathtaking development in so many ways for

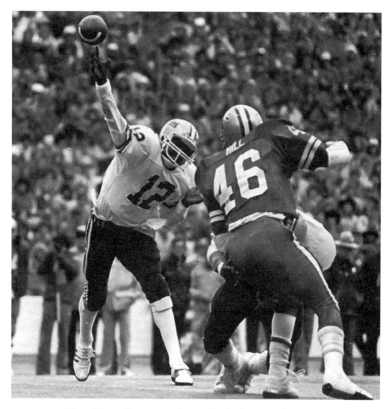

After Clete Casper got hurt, Ricky Turner (12) came
on and did his best, but the Apple Cup loss of 1981, which
kept us out of the Rose Bowl, was one of the most painful ever.
(Photo courtesy of Washington State University)

us, but we were shooting for the whole works. We wanted the Rose Bowl... and Washington denied us.

This was a game I strongly felt we could win, but two developments swung the other way early. Quarterback Clete Casper pulled a hamstring early in the second quarter. He was a stable leader who could operate the offense in that hostile environment. As good as Ricky Turner was, he wasn't quite ready; he was just too young to handle that Husky Stadium crowd. And once we got behind, it was tougher to try to make up points with our running quarterback instead of our passer.

I think Clete's untimely injury kept us out of the Rose Bowl, but there was also a play with just eight seconds left in the first half that killed our momentum. Our Nate Bradley was in position to pick off a Steve Pelluer pass right in the corner of the end zone. We were ahead 7-3 at the time. It was raining, of course, and the turf was wet. As Nate started to take off on a little jump to get the ball, both his feet went out from under him. Instead of lifting off, he slipped, and when he went down, Paul Skansi made a nice adjustment to the ball and pulled it in for a touchdown. That was a huge turnaround, going from what seemed to be a sure pick, or at least a knock-down, to a touchdown. Instead of going into halftime ahead 7-3, we were down 10-7 with momentum flowing in their direction.

They ran the ball well, with Cookie Jackson and Jacque Robinson totaling about 200 yards between them. We ended up losing 23-10. This was one of the rare Apple Cups when we came into the game with a higher ranking. At 8-1-1, we were 14th, while the 8-2 Huskies were 17th. We knew we were getting better. We had a great season, and the Holiday Bowl was a nice painkiller, but, man, that Apple Cup loss hurt.

To have been able to hold on and make it to the Rose Bowl might have profoundly changed the course of the future for Cougar football.

BED CHECK FORGERY

When we got invited to the 1981 Holiday Bowl, we were all determined we were going to San Diego to have a good time. Athletic director Sam Jankovich said that this school hadn't been to a bowl in 51 years, so let's enjoy it and maybe the carry-over will be that the players come to see that this kind of thing is worth working and fighting for.

It was a wonderful experience, and we intentionally had a loose rein on the kids. We told them that it was going to be pretty much an on-your-own mentality the first three nights. But at the very least we wanted everybody to check in by 2 a.m. and sign their names, along with the time they got in, on a legal pad we had set out. That way we could pick it up and count the numbers and make sure everybody was accounted for.

I gave them that I-know-I-can-trust-you speech. Yeah, sure. But, you know what, I didn't come to the Holiday Bowl to kick kids off the team. Every morning, somebody would bring me the list to take a look at, and right away I saw that all 90 guys were in on time... but at least 60 of the names were signed in the same handwriting.

I just laughed. Never said a word.

Our grad assistant at the time was Tom Osborne, who went on to be a wonderful coach and have a great career at Portland State, Boise State, Oregon and Arizona State. His nickname was "Unimportant Tom" because the "important" Tom Osborne was at Nebraska.

At least 10 years went by and one night I asked Tom, as an established coach, if he ever found himself with a grad assistant who faked players' signatures on the bed-check list. He turned all red and asked how long I had known about it.

"Uh, since the first morning you handed me the list, Tom."

What a great time we had in San Diego. Sam made sure everything we did was first-cabin, and we all had fun. A little bit too much, maybe. We were way down at halftime and I told them that this had been a great trip, but anytime they decided to start playing a little football would be fine with me. They surely did, and BYU had to hang on to win, 38-36.

JIM McMAHON

Losing the '81 Holiday Bowl had more to do with Jim McMahon quarterbacking a good BYU team than us not being ready for the game. In a strict football sense, passing teams like BYU have an easier time getting back in rhythm after a six-week layoff than running teams do. You can always go out and throw the ball around, but the running game requires timing that is hard to replicate during practice.

There's no question that Jim McMahon could play. But he didn't win a lot of friends that week among the WSU Cougars in San Diego; our kids really disliked him. In fairness, BYU had been to three straight Holiday Bowls as the champs of the Western Athletic Conference, so to McMahon, everything seemed old hat. We'd go to the zoo or to see Shamu, and he'd be over there leaning back like he was half-asleep. The worst thing was at the luncheon we had aboard the U.S.S. *Kitty Hawk*. He was at the head table laying down his head on folded arms like he was sleeping. It was totally disrespectful.

After the game, one of the reporters asked our defensive tackle Ken Collins about the experience. He said: "The time we had was wonderful, in fact, the only negative thing about the whole experience is that Jim McMahon was the biggest asshole I've ever seen."

I called Ken later and told him that he should try to do a better job of watching his language. But I didn't get on him too much because I knew how he felt. You have to give McMahon credit, though, he was an athlete and he made a lot of plays. Late in the game on a fourth-and-one, they went for it at midfield and he fumbled the snap. He had the presence of mind to reach down and get it and dive for the first down by about four inches.

None of that changed the opinion of a lot of Cougars, though, who saw him just the way Ken Collins did.

MYTHS DEBUNKED

Yes, BYU beat us 38-36 in that 1981 Holiday Bowl. But it had been since January 1, 1931 that a Washington State football team had been to a bowl game, any bowl game, and just getting invited was critical to our development. The true and long-lasting part of that was the way it broke down a barrier, and showed Cougar players from then on that something like that could be accomplished.

You've got to remember, bowls were hard to come by back then. They didn't have 28 of them, or however many they have now. There were only a dozen or so, and you really had to be good to get into one of them. Remember, too, that we came within an eyelash that season of getting to the Rose Bowl, something that no Cougar fan alive ever truly believed was a possibility. We came so close, we had the fumble against UCLA while we were trying to just run out the clock that led to a tie, and then of course, we lived through the heartbreak of losing such a significant Apple Cup that year.

Going to that bowl game resonated very strongly throughout the Cougar Kingdom that something like this was possible. From then on, recruits could believe they could get to a bowl by being a Cougar. All those myths that surrounded Washington State evaporated. That was an enormous turn-around for us.

CHAPTER 7

MAKING BETTER COUGARS

SELF-IMPROVEMENT CLASSES

Nobody ever accused me of running a finishing school at Washington State, but I was absolutely serious about trying to help our guys with their manners and conduct, and understanding the rules of acceptable social behavior. These men were important representatives of the university and the community, and I felt they needed to know how to act.

Every Sunday after home games, we'd have film study at 4 p.m., but before that, I'd bring the team together and we'd talk about a litany of things that had nothing to do with football. We'd discuss things they might have to deal with in social situations, things that I hoped would make them better people. We'd talk about the importance of reading, writing legibly, of manners, courtesy, respect. It was a free-form class and they could say anything they wanted, so somebody was always busting somebody's chops because there's some great comics on every football team. I was sure the time we spent on this brought us all closer together.

What I'd seen was that nobody teaches young people some of these important things they should be using every day. I saw a bunch of guys who knew about as much about social behavior as I knew of geology. I thought it was part of my job to help them out. What side of the lady should you be on if you're walking down the sidewalk? Where do you put your napkin when you leave a table? You don't just toss it in the gravy. Which fork do you use? How do you dress for an interview?

In a world filled with bad language, do you have to swear? Can't you be more conscious of your language? Are you acting like your grandmother is watching? That's one I used to talk to them about all the time. Would you want your grandmother to hear you cussin' a blue streak?

We would have somebody come in from a men's store in town and show them how to dress. He'd bring a sports coat and a suit and some interchangeable pants to show them how they could look nice on a budget.

We'd talk about money. I'd have a show of hands: How many of you have bank accounts? How many have written a check? You wouldn't believe it, but we'd find out that half the team hadn't established bank accounts. So we'd talk about how to do that, and how to handle the checkbook. Nobody had ever taken the time to teach some of these kids such important basics to everyday life.

We'd talk about how to do interviews with media guys. How to stop repeatedly saying "Ya know?" How you could be a strong Christian without starting every answer in an interview having to thank God as your Personal Savior. Your message can get lost if you pound people too hard with it.

Mostly, it was about how to be a gentleman, how to be respectful. As it turned out, the benefits went a long way. It's shocking how many guys told me later how much that meant to them. Some of them thanked me for having saved them some embarrassment because they had never learned some of these things. I also had many parents over the years tell me how important it was to them that we took the time to do it.

I know we had a ball with it. I got into this business to be a teacher and I saw that our guys needed this. I'm sure players need it every bit as much now. Maybe even more than ever. I think every program should have somebody doing this. It's best with a head coach conducting the classes, though, because at least they had to "act" like they were paying attention to me.

OUTTA THE WAY, BUDDY

The only time our self-improvement classes didn't bear positive results was when I gave them all an assignment for the week: To work on stepping aside and opening doors for ladies as they were heading into a class room or the student union. It was the right thing to do, besides, that one small gesture, alone, would create a better image of the football team on campus.

Almost everybody said they earned compliments from the women. One poor guy, in a time when women's liberation was becoming more forceful, said "Coach, I did exactly like you told me and I opened the door for this woman, but she started swearing at me about how she could get the damned door for herself without the help of any damned football player." Here he's trying to be a good guy and he got his butt ripped for it. Otherwise, the results were always very positive, and it feels good to think there may be a large group of well-mannered former Cougar players out there.

FOR WHAT IT'S WORTH

Some critics contend that college athletes are spoiled and have no understanding of how fortunate they are. Well, then, it's up to us to teach them. I thought it was important for them to know what their scholarship was worth, so, in our self-improvement classes, I used to have a session breaking down the economics of their scholarship.

We would list the expenses, how much it cost to get them through admissions, room and board, books. Back then, it was something like $8,000 a year, and there were 90 of them, so that's $700,000 just to get them through registration. Then we feed them, house them, outfit them. You could see them start to sit up and pay attention as the money total grew.

Then we'd go through some of the other expenses. After all the costs to keep football going, they had to realize there were 18 sports at the school, and 16 of them didn't make a dime, in fact, they lost money. I'd go through the budget lines and show them… tennis, gymnastics, swimming, these sports have these expenses.

I thought it was important for them to see not only how much they were getting from the university, but how much they were giving back, too. There was a strong need to know that they were helping men and women athletes in some of those other sports compete and get college educations just like they were. After we did this, I don't think I ever heard any of that grumbling about the university making millions and the football players getting nothing but a little, crummy scholarship in return.

AGENTS OF CHANGE

I'm one of the coaches who don't consider "agents" a dirty word. They have a job to do. But it was important that they never got in the way of the job we were trying to do. My first case dealing with them came during our 1978 trip to West Point to play Army. We flew in on Friday and had a block of rooms at a Holiday Inn. Not long after we settled in, I got a call from Steve Grant, Jack Thompson's roommate. He said, "Coach, there's an agent in our room making a pitch to Jack."

I got right down there and it turned out this guy must have bribed the motel clerk to let him have a room right next to Jack's. Agents knew no quarter in those days, and they'd even try to talk to your players as they were walking onto the field. I told him to get out because we had a game we had to prepare for.

I saw then that these guys were going to become an issue if I didn't develop some kind of policy. From then on, I would help screen these guys. As pro prospects started getting information from agents, I had them bring it to me and we went through it. He would pick maybe his top three candidates, and I would write or call them to set up meetings where they could make their pitches in an orderly fashion.

I wasn't going to tell them who to pick, of course, but I was going to do whatever I could to make sure there weren't any shenanigans that would exploit the player, or anything that would disrupt the rest of the team. It made the agent know that he was going to go through me and we weren't going to allow unprofessional behavior. Some agents told me afterward that they appreciated it and wished it were done that way at all colleges.

MAKING THE GRADE

We never had a Rhodes Scholar, but we had several who won National Football Foundation scholarships for academic excellence, and we certainly had a number of players who went on to be very successful and productive as doctors, lawyers, accountants and the like.

I used to say that you can't ever recruit a kid who is too smart... but, believe me, there is a minimal threshold on the bottom end. The paradox was that sometimes you had really intelligent kids who weren't good students of the game.

At times I'd get frustrated with some of the great students on the football field because they needed things in a logical order. Football isn't a question-and-answer thought process, football is reactionary. Some of the smarter kids would want to stop and think out a Plan B when Plan A broke down, whereas some of those mediocre students were pretty accustomed to wheeling and dealing and learning to improvise since they were always having to move on to Plan B or Plan C.

Defensive lineman Greg Porter may have been one of the very best students we had, with almost a 4-point every year. He went on to be a very successful accountant, and the great thing about him was he had terrific brain power, but also some good functional common sense on the field, too.

CAP AND GOWN CREW

Every coach must be held accountable for the finished product... the student as he completes the program. But I object to the NCAA's formula for computing graduation rates, which is based on the progress of the group of incoming freshmen.

I think what should count is the number of guys who graduate after exhausting their eligibility. There are a million reasons why kids leave programs after their freshman year. A coach has no control over guys who quit because of marriage or injuries or a death in the family, or homesickness... you name it. But they count against you in the typical graduation-rate mathematics.

A perfect example involves a couple basketball players who started at Washington and then transferred to Gonzaga, where they graduated with honors. The way the NCAA adds it up, Washington is penalized for those two, but Gonzaga gets no credit because those kids didn't come in with a freshman class. That's ridiculous; here's a couple honors graduates who are forever lost in that shuffle of numbers.

I always wanted to be responsible for the kids who got to the end of the race with me. How did they do? I've added them up. My '86 group graduated 19 of 23, and over the nine years, 116 of 162 graduated. That's almost 72 percent, and I've got reason to believe that some of those have gone on and worked for degrees later on. I truly am proud of that.

TWO-PERCENT RULE

In nine seasons at Washington State, I released 21 players. And when I say released, I mean "kicked off." That's not too many, nine years, 90 guys on a team… a little more than two per year. I used to tell them when they got together that there probably would be two percent of them whose chairs were going to be empty. Don't be part of that two percent, I'd warn.

If somebody was involved in drugs, it was automatic dismissal. Stealing, fighting, that sort of thing, you'd probably get a second strike. Lack of academic progress was always real trouble. Anything that had to do with mistreatment of women was dealt with immediately, I wouldn't tolerate that, and they knew it. If I had a complaint from a girl on campus, we got to that in a hurry. As much as you fight against it, there's a persistent image of football players as ruffians. No matter how many are on their way to becoming doctors or architects, they still carried that image as ruffians. You had to try to protect a positive image of football players, and you certainly had to make it clear that women were safe on campus from football players.

Over time, some guys don't shape up and, frankly, you get tired of feeding them. I thought that being on scholarship obliged you to try to improve yourself mentally and physically. If you showed a history of missing classes, not putting in effort, then we had a chat. If that showed no results, then the second chat was something more harsh.

But I never took away a guy's scholarship for a lack of talent. If they worked and filled their obligations, they were fine with me. At times I would call kids in, just for the sake of being honest and up front with them. I might tell them, as it looked, there was a good chance of them not playing much. Your scholarship is safe; we committed that to you. And we'll try to work you in on special teams or whatever we can do. But if you have aspirations of being a starting player, you may need to drop down a notch. I think kids appreciated that.

WALDENISM

Without a doubt, women are the No. 1 problem of a college football coach. It's not their fault, but they inadvertently create more problems on a football team than any other single thing. Dating, getting into trouble, breaking up, heartache, homesickness, guys getting into fights over them. There's nothing even close to the impact that women have on football players.

CHAPTER 8

IN THE DOGHOUSE... AGAIN

THE WALDEN RELEASE

My big mouth got me in a little trouble a few times. Okay, maybe more than a few times, and maybe more than a little trouble, too. In fact, it was such a steady occurrence that President Terrell learned to deal with it swiftly and efficiently.

He told me that he had formatted a document he called "The Walden Release." He had some printed up and ready for distribution. It said something like: "The words and opinions of Coach Jim Walden do not necessarily reflect the position or policies of Washington State University or its administration."

Some days, after I'd opened my mouth too much, I could almost hear them up on the hill screaming: "Put out the Walden Release!"

SIMIAN STATESMEN

I guess the biggest thing I got in trouble for was when I blasted the State Legislature over some funding issues. I think I said something like: "You can't have athletics being tied to a bunch of monkeys in the Legislature." Even President Terrell winced a little bit when he heard that one. Crank out The Walden Release.

ON THE CARPET

Most of the time my opinions only created small waves. One time, however, I got called in by the Pac-10 honchos to face a committee over comments I made about USC. They had been on probation for doing some pretty bad things. But somehow, in the middle of a two-year bowl suspension, they got let out of jail and had the second year of the suspension deferred so they could go to a bowl.

I just pitched a fit. You can't do that. I said something about how wrong it was to let the crooks out of jail so they could go take a vacation on a mountain top. I thought that was unfair to the rest of the teams in the league. If you've caught a team cheating, you can't just all of a sudden forget about it. Let's just say I took issue with their judgment. Maybe they were a little concerned about me using the word "crooks" to apply to one of their flagship franchises.

Of course, this is exactly what I told the committee. They said that I should not have said something like that in the press and that I should have taken it through the proper channels.

Okay, you can probably read my lips, I was about to call BS on this official. I had a few words with these fine gentlemen over the years. But I was never afraid to speak my mind on the sidelines or in the media… and I could live with whatever hot water it got me into. (Photo courtesy of Washington State University)

That got me worked up; I argued that if they had handled the situation the way they should have in the first place, USC wouldn't have been paroled to play in the bowl game. Well, they didn't like hearing that much.

Dr. Terrell could see how this was going and handled it beautifully. I'll never forget it, he very calmly said: "Now, Jim, maybe it will be better if I do most of the talking from this point."

SEEMED LIKE A GOOD IDEA

Maybe some considered the Great Bumper Sticker Caper an act of widespread vandalism, but I prefer to see it as an admirably aggressive, grassroots marketing campaign.

Every time I went over to Seattle, I'd get stuck in traffic behind somebody with a "Husky Fever" bumper sticker on the car. Man, I can't even express how sick I got of looking at those things. I got the idea that there's a ton of Cougar fans in King County and the Tacoma area, and we should be able to counterattack with bumper stickers of our own. I went out one summer and promoted "Go Cougars" bumper stickers on the theory that nothing would be more infuriating for Husky fans to suddenly start finding themselves stuck in traffic behind Cougar fans. We felt it was good advertisement for us.

It then crossed my mind that we might be able to take it a step further. I looked around and figured there must be something like 6,000 cars on the campus in Pullman, and the bulk of them belonged to students who are from the west side of the state. So, out of my own pocket, I bought about 5,000 of these bumper stickers. I financed it because if we ended up in hot water, the responsibility would be mine alone and I'd stand up for it.

Now, keep in mind, players are devious. If you said, "Let's go steal some watermelons," the whole team would volunteer. If you said, "Let's go to church," then 72 percent had just developed a nagging cough. I told them, I've got this great idea: I'll divide up the campus into sections and assign you all different parking lots. We'll go out at dawn and start putting these things on the cars. I was real strict about how they were to do it: Don't put it on painted surfaces and only on that rear bumper on the passenger side. I had them all carrying garbage bags because I didn't want them littering with that paper backing they'd have to rip off every sticker. I sent the commandos out before daybreak so they could be done and gone before anybody got up for class.

By noon, I had 100 complaints. The police called. Dick Young, my athletic director, called. Of course, a meeting followed. There was a big rigamarole, of course. What were you thinking, Jim? I thought, hey, I'm giving them away free. I'm providing a service. Why would a student on this campus object to having a free "Go Cougars" bumper sticker?

Yeah, I caught some flak about it, but it died down in a couple days. These bumper stickers are still out there, though. Every time I see one now… I just smile.

WALDENISM

Sometimes I wished I wouldn't have said some of the things that have gotten me in trouble over the years. But it wasn't my fault, somebody was always calling and asking me for my opinion. Can't blame me for that… they shouldn't call me if they didn't want to hear what I had to say.

CHAPTER 9

OVERWHELMING UPSETS

APPLE CUP '82: OVERWHELMING

The Washington Huskies had not visited our campus for 28 seasons. But it's unlikely that many thought that would make much difference to a great Washington team with Jacque Robinson running the ball, Steve Pelluer passing to Paul Skansi, and Chuck Nelson kicking flawlessly. When we walked onto that field, we were heavy, heavy underdogs. They had gone to two straight Rose Bowls and were looking forward to a third. They were 9-1, had been ranked No. 1 in the country most of the season, and were still No. 5 as they found their way over to Pullman. On the other hand, we had been banged up all season and had just two wins and a tie on the record.

But we felt it was a little like sabotage… we were really hidin' in the bushes. We had lost an unbelievable number of players to injury early in the year, but come late October, some of those guys we were counting on started creeping back. It meant we had a much better team at Apple Cup time than we'd had all season, and I imagine we were a whole lot better than Washington thought we were.

The biggest factor, though, was simply playing the Huskies in Pullman, which an entire generation of Cougar fans had never seen. Just think about that. We finally had a home-field advantage. I'll admit I played this up a little in the press, with this quote: "... They have to be careful because we're loose as a goose, and they sure stand to lose a heckuva lot more than we do." Hey, it couldn't hurt to plant a seed of doubt.

On Friday before the game, I was laughing. I knew how organized Don James was, and that meant that this was a new problem for him to face. I knew he had to spend time developing a thought process on this one. How do we get to Pullman? Where's the hotel? What do you mean our hotel is in Idaho? They were dealing with a lot of unknowns. It was an uncomfortable position that none of those coaches or players had ever been in, and the unknown can be really disconcerting.

We were down at halftime, yet I had this feeling we were going to win it. The enthusiasm in the stadium was beyond anything I'd heard in my life. We came out and went down and scored, and from that point on, it just went berserk in that place. It was overwhelming.

Maybe the most memorable play, and one that I know shocked a lot of Huskies, was Nelson's field-goal attempt with about four minutes left. We were leading 21-20 and Nelson lined up for a 33-yarder. He had made an NCAA record of 30 straight, and the Huskies had beaten us eight times. He missed, and both those streaks ended that day. We won, 24-20. And the goal posts, I'm told, ended up in the Palouse River.

I've always been guilty of getting a little carried away, but this time it was for good reason. What a great moment, winning the Apple Cup of 1982. The Huskies finally had to come to play us in Pullman, and I know that our fans and that stadium were huge parts of that win.
(*Bart Rayniak/*The Spokesman-Review)

I'll never forget a quote in the Sunday morning paper by a Husky after we beat them. He said, "I never thought this would happen in my lifetime." Think about that. He was 22 years old, and he thought they were going to go another 50 years without losing to us.

That's how deeply ingrained was the notion of Husky superiority in the Apple Cup. Changing that mentality, for us, was the biggest challenge of our careers. Playing that game in Pullman, I know, made a huge difference. I know for a fact that Don didn't like coming over to Pullman, but from then on, that was how it was going to be. Playing them on the road was one thing, but having our home games on a neutral field just wasn't going to happen anymore.

THE HAUNTING MISS

When Don James sent Chuck Nelson onto the field for that last field goal attempt, I was so certain he'd make it that I didn't even bother to watch. I had so much respect for him, I just left my normal spot on the sidelines because I felt there was no chance he could ever miss from there. I made the assumption that we were going to be down 23-21, and I went down to the offensive end of the bench and was talking to players and coaches about our timeout situation and how far we needed to go to get into field-goal range to win it.

All of a sudden, I heard this huge roar from the crowd. I'd been at this long enough to know that when the crowd in Pullman screams like that, it has to be something good for us. I whirled and looked and our players were going berserk; they couldn't believe it. Chuck Nelson had missed the kick.

I have thought of this so many times, for all the great things he did for Washington, for all the incredible kicks he made for the Huskies over the years, Chuck Nelson should never have to bear the blame for that one miss. There are so many things that happen in a game that determine the outcome... not just one kick. He was one of the all-time great kickers and it's unfair for fans to forget all the kicks he made and remember only the one he didn't.

PRESIDENT'S PEP TALK

In my heart, I had believed that I truly had pushed my teams to understand the importance of the Apple Cup. But I got a pep talk before the 1982 game that took me up another notch. And I think it was crucial to our success against the Huskies that week.

After the Cal game the week before, I got a call from President Terrell asking me if I'd stop by for a visit on Sunday. He said he wanted to talk about the Apple Cup game. Now, getting called in by the president makes you a little nervous. He gave me one of the most impassioned speeches on why it was so important, from his perspective, to get the job done against Washington.

He told me how tired he gets of going to the Board of Regents meetings and dealing with the perception that he was the president from "the other school" in the state. He talked about the importance of people—from regents to alums—having respect for this university. It was very emotional and it really got to me. I'll tell you what, it made it very clear that I had to do a better job of inspiring my players exactly the way he had inspired me.

The first thing I did was have a staff meeting and I really laid into my coaches. THIS HAS GOT TO STOP! We have got to put an end to this. We have got to get it through to our players how important this is. We have to reach deeper, we have to reach them and motivate them, and get them to understand that we've got to stop being second-class citizens in this game.

Man, we got after it like you can't believe. I came away thinking what a great man President Terrell was. He'd had to endure the losses for eight straight years. His talk made me want to win that game so badly. And when we did, I was never more emotionally drained in my life.

He called the next morning; he expressed great satisfaction.

CLETE CASPER

Neither Clete Casper nor Ricky Turner ever really liked it when I alternated them at quarterback in the early '80s. I don't blame them, I wouldn't have either. It's hard on the ego. But they lived with it, and it worked pretty well for us.

Clete was one of my favorite quarterbacks, and was one of the first top-notch athletes from the west side to commit to us. He had a great arm, but probably couldn't break 5.1 in the 40-yard dash. He had such a wonderful understanding of the game, and because of that I felt he was one of the few quarterbacks who could have called his own plays.

Clete Casper and Ricky Turner were our tag-team quarterbacks for a while, and it was a productive twosome as Clete had a great arm and Ricky had terrific feet. Clete, getting off a pass here against UCLA, had a true grasp of what it took to run our offense.
(Photo courtesy of Washington State University)

Of course, we used one quarterback to set up the other one, and Clete actually had to sacrifice more than Ricky did because Ricky was younger and knew he had more time to play. We would see some of the passing game open up for Clete because of Ricky running the option, and some of the option stuff would be effective for Ricky because of Clete's passing. Clete did a wonderful job of directing our offense, and Ricky could get white hot and could break anything for a big gain. It gave us a great one-two punch.

KEITH MILLARD

Keith Millard went on to have a very productive career in the NFL, and is a tremendous guy with a great family. But one thing you never wanted to do, when he was at Washington State, was get between him and a pizza.

His reputation was that he was a troublemaker, although I think it was mostly an erroneous reputation based on one incident. One night he was leaving a fraternity house and had too much to drink, which was not a good thing for Keith. On the way out, he bumped into a pizza-delivery guy, which was bad timing for a guy trying to sneak a pizza past a hungry Keith Millard.

Keith is this huge guy with a real deep voice, and as the story goes, he asked the delivery kid for a couple pieces of pizza. Of course he couldn't give him any since he was taking it to somebody else and he couldn't show up with only part of a pizza. So, Keith wasn't very happy about that and conked him right on the top of the head. The guy went down. Supposedly, Keith checked to make sure he was okay, laid the

Keith Millard (93) put a lot of pressure on opposing quarterbacks, and a little bit on his coach, too, until he settled down and turned into a disciplined player and student. (Photo courtesy of Washington State University)

pizza box flat out on the guy's chest, took out a couple pieces, closed the lid and went on his way.

About 2 in the morning I get this call from campus police that they were going to arrest Keith. Oh, great. We came down on him hard. Our part of his punishment was our famed "20-mile Week." For two months, he had to get up at 5 a.m., four days a week. We hauled him out to the Moscow-Pullman airport and made him run back to campus. That's about five miles. Rain, snow, didn't matter, weather was not a condition, you ran in anything.

It was our toughest discipline short of being kicked off the team. And once the team got wind of it, we didn't have to use it very often. Keith was never a problem for us after that. He was always eligible and always went to class. He had some troubles in the NFL, but he's a tremendous guy who seems really squared away and has a nice career going as a coach in the NFL.

SLOW START, BIG FINISH

For a long time, we had to battle our own state of mind as well as opponents on the field. Even when we were good, we sometimes lost a few games before the kids really believed how good we could be. When you've been down and taken some beatings, it's human nature to be skeptical. The magazines and media played a part in it, too. Washington State players would read in all those magazines that they were going to finish eighth or ninth in the conference. And when you try to convince them how good they are, you're struggling against everybody else who is putting doubts in their minds.

That doesn't happen at USC. If they were bringing back the same guys we had, they'd be ranked second or third. They'd go to the newsstand and say, "Hey, lookie here, we're gonna be real good again this season."

We tied for second in the conference in 1981, and I can guarantee you that we were picked eighth in 1982. That sort of thing affects your summer workouts and fall camp and the early part of the season. You're always playing against a level of low expectations that somebody else has created. In 1983, we had one of the great defenses, with Ricky Reynolds, Keith Millard, Erik Howard, Eric Williams, Junior Tupuola, Milford Hodge, Rico Tipton... and a bunch of other really good players. But we went 2-4 before we figured out how good we were and won the last five games of the season.

We played one of the best teams in America, a Michigan club that finished No. 9 in the country, and we were ahead 17-14 in front of 103,000 of their fans. Near the end, our free safety got hurt, and they ran a power-pitch and our substitute didn't get over there to fill. They went up 20-17.

Mark Rypien drove us down the field with less than three minutes left and he barely overthrew a wide-open receiver in the end zone; it was windy and the ball just took off on him a little bit. We lined up to kick the game-tying field goal and we missed it.

Now, that should have told us that we're a pretty good football team. Finally, we got through to them and ran past the last five opponents. In the last four games, nobody scored more than nine points against us, and we shut down Washington 17-6 on the road.

You look back and we were 7-4 and finished alone at third in the conference at 5-3. But back then, there wasn't a bowl game for us. That should have been our second bowl game in three seasons, and, the way things are now, we'd have gone

again in '84. I know that could have done nothing but help
our program.

JUNIOR ACHIEVEMENT

Headaches and gratification ran neck and neck when dealing with linebacker Junior Tupuola, although I've never
coached a more interesting character or personality in all my
years. He was a tremendous football player, for one thing. But
if there was ever a guy who could be classified as a true Dennis
the Menace, it was Junior.

This guy could dance like you wouldn't believe, so every
girl in town wanted to dance with him. Which, of course, led
to problems. He could do that moonwalk thing that Michael
Jackson does, but even better. With Junior, though, it was
always one thing after another. Nothing big, but always being
at somebody's fraternity house or someplace he shouldn't be.
Not in jail, but just Peck's Bad Boy troubles.

So, I'd kick him off the team about once a year, but then
I'd miss him so much, because he was such a great kid, that I'd
always bring him back. I had to initiate what I called a "Junior
Alert," whereby I told all the players that whenever they saw
him in town or at a party to tell him that Coach Walden was
about to show up. Just to keep him on his toes.

But he was such a fun character and such a great young
man that he'd come back in my office with those big, sad eyes
and tell me he'd never get in trouble again. Yes, you will. No,
I won't. Yes, you will. Okay, maybe. I will say that Junior
Tupuola got more of my attention than any other three guys

Junior Tupuola (54), one of my all-time favorite Cougars, picks off a pass here for us. For all the headaches he gave us off the field, it's funny to note that he's now Rev. Tupuola. (Photo courtesy of Washington State University)

the whole time I was at Washington State. Was it worth the effort?

Here's what makes the story so good. Nobody was more of a renegade and at-risk guy than Junior. But today, he's a minister on the island of Samoa. I always tell him that nobody can spread the word of the Lord like Junior because nobody's had to worry about the wrath as much as Junior.

FRIGHTENING MOMENT

Junior Tupuola may have been led to the ministry after one potentially lethal incident when it seemed that only divine assistance could help him out. Trouble seemed to land at the feet of Junior. In one case, it arrived in the form of a pistol.

The team had just barely arrived on campus and gone through physicals when Junior hooked a ride to the chow hall from Rod Retherford. Rod was an old farm boy from over near Pendleton, Oregon, great kid, never an ounce of trouble. He'd apparently forgotten that under his car seat he had kept, over the summer, what he called his varmint pistol. It was a little .22 that he used around the ranch for shooting groundhogs or whatever.

He took off in the car and this gun slid out from under the seat into the hands of Junior Tupuola, who was sitting behind Rod. Not knowing anything about guns, he picked it up, and as he said, "Is this thing loaded?" it went off. I was in Bohler Gym and somebody came in shouting, "Junior Tupuola just shot Rod Retherford." Not, "There's been an accident," or anything like that.

I got to the hospital in a panic. Rod was asking if he was going to live or die, and Junior was white as the bed sheet. By some miracle, the bullet went in his neck and didn't do any long-term damage; Rod was able to come back and play defensive back for us.

APPLE CUP '83: SATISFYING

This was one year when we were better than Washington and we played that way, holding the Huskies to two field goals and winning 17-6. It was one of our most satisfying wins because of the way it validated the Apple Cup win the previous year. There'd been so much hoopla about us denying them the Rose Bowl that it seemed almost an insult to us, as if that somehow hurt them so much more than it hurt us the year before when they knocked us out of the Rose Bowl.

I knew we had a good team in '83, and it was special because it was the best defensive team I ever had, without a doubt. The defense wasn't just talented, it had the kind of attitude you wish every team could develop.

Here's an example. We fumbled on the first play of the game and they recovered on our 20. In three plays, they made just four yards and they had to settle for a Jeff Jaeger field goal. That defense was determined to give up nothing.

After that field goal, defensive lineman Keith Millard came running off the field right at me. You can tell when somebody is coming at you with something on his mind, and he was headed right for me. He didn't stop until he got maybe six inches from my nose. You never see this; players just never crowd a coach like that. But Keith took off his helmet and got right in my face, looked me in the eye and said: "Coach, don't sweat it, we're kickin' their ass." I thought, okay, big boy, whatever you say. That's the kind of attitude they had.

We dominated the game. We ran the ball so well, with Kerry Porter picking up 169 yards, that Ricky Turner had to throw only 10 passes. We were good and we knew we were good. Keith Millard would have told you that.

WALDENISM

You can't compare teams from different eras. You used to have to be good to get into a bowl game. If they'd had the 30 bowl games they do now, we'd have gone in 1981, '83 and '84. I don't know how dramatically that would have changed anything, except I know it would have been a lot more fun and would have been good for our program. I know at least that we wouldn't have heard the criticism that we couldn't get a bowl bid.

CHAPTER 10

OPPOSING COACHES

JOE KAPP

Joe Kapp brought his reputation as a great player back to the California Bears with him, but he didn't bring along any experience as a coach. That situation made it difficult for him and led to some resentment among the rest of the league's coaches.

I had known Joe for a long time and considered him a friend. We had played in the Canadian Football League together, and we were even traded for each other one time. When Joe got the job at Cal in 1982, I wrote him a note congratulating him. A couple months later, I got a call from Joe telling me he felt as if he received something less than a warm welcome from the league's coaches.

Fact was, he wasn't welcomed, except by me. I already knew him, but even I wasn't very happy about the situation. I explained to him that he was a threat to the existence of every coach who had spent years and years working his way up. Joe had never even diagrammed a huddle, but because he was a well-known former star player, he got the job as Cal's coach.

A lot of us had coached for years hoping to one day get that big break, and he'd done none of that. If he came in off the street and was successful, it would mean that every fan in the stands was right; heck, anybody can do this job. Every school was going to just go out and hire a big-name alum to come back and run the team.

I explained to him all those reasons why he was not going to be warmly received. He said he figured something was up because nobody would trade films with him. Well, of course not, Joe, what can you share with them, films of last year's team when somebody else was the coach? What good is that going to do them? They're not going to show you everything they do and not get anything in return.

Now, I was a little different. That first year we didn't play them until the 10th game, and some of the teams he was playing before us, well, I just plain didn't like them very much. So, I sent him all kinds of film. I had to tell him straight out, though, if I had to play him in the first couple weeks of the season, I wouldn't have given him anything, either.

To be honest, I worried about him succeeding, too. I thought he was a friend and we had a rapport and I respected him. I knew his heart was in the right place; he loved his school. But for him to be successful would have been a slap in the face of the guys who worked so hard for so many years. He was a good guy... but he hadn't earned his spurs.

JOE CAP

A bitter cold rain was falling, and it looked like we were in for a miserable day on the sidelines of our game against Cal in Pullman one season. Without really thinking about it, I grabbed a wool hat that looked like it would keep the rain off my head, and I went onto the field for pregame warm-ups. What I didn't notice was that the hat that I picked up was one that belonged to my son Murray. It had a USC logo on it.

Cal coach Joe Kapp absolutely hated USC. It came with the territory, I guess. If you coached at Cal, you hated USC. Those folks had not been too kind to him when he came into coaching, anyway.

We met on the field before the game to shoot the breeze a little bit, and he said: "Are you doin' this just to make me mad?" I had no idea what he was talking about. Doing what? "Wearing that blankety-blank USC hat… you know how badly I hate those sons-a-bitches." He scalded me for a while. Joe, I'm just tryin' to keep my head dry, I didn't even notice what kind of hat it was. He didn't seem to want to believe me. Funny thing, none of my players or assistants said a word to me about the hat.

USC'S '79 POWERHOUSE

As much as every coach strives to pull off even the most unlikely upset, realistically, we didn't have much chance when we came up against USC at the Los Angeles Coliseum on October 6, 1979. Against the No. 1-ranked and defending national champion Trojans, we eventually got beat 51-21. But I almost brokered a much narrower margin before the coin toss.

It was one of those gorgeous southern California days, and the Trojans were a magnificent football team, maybe among the best in the history of the game. Eleven guys on that team would go on to be first-round draft picks—imagine that. They had Anthony Munoz, Brad Budde, Charles White, Ronnie Lott, Dennis Smith, Chip Banks, Marcus Allen, Joey Browner,

Don Mosebar and a ton of other great players over there. They'd won the '78 title and were on a streak of winning 19 of 20 games.

Tough task for the Cougs, in other words. I'd watched the films, of course, but I really knew we were in trouble when our buses pulled up to the Coliseum and theirs came in right after us. I decided to have our team stay aboard and let USC get off first. Big mistake. As they walked past, all their guys were looking in our windows. Do you know how high the windows are on a bus? Their guys were so big they didn't even have to get on their tippy-toes to see in. Might have scared the wits out of half our guys.

Coach John Robinson and I were on the field before the game shooting the bull a little bit, and the officials came over to us to check on our teams' equipment. The rule then was that everybody had to have certified helmets and standard equipment, or you could face forfeiture of the game. The referee asked Coach Robby about the equipment and he said, "Yes, we're fine." Then he turned to me and asked if our players had the standard equipment as per NCAA regulations.

"You know, fact is, we really don't," I told him. "We're not like Southern Cal; at Washington State, we've got an itty-bitty budget and we just can't afford to throw away 100 helmets this year and replace them all to be in compliance. But we'll make do."

The referee and Coach Robby just stared at me. The official had to be thinking, "Oh, no, don't do this to me, please don't do this."

They kept staring, but I never cracked a smile.

"Look, my guys will be fine, heck, they don't hit that hard anyway, they won't get hurt. Mr. Official, I'm afraid you're going to have to call this a forfeit. And as I recall, a forfeit is recorded as a 6-0 loss, which would suit me just fine."

Robby broke up… "Gosh dang it, Jim."

Well, we had the equipment. But they had the horses. They were up something like 45-0 at the half, which had me thinking how good a 6-0 loss would have looked. Hey, we might have picked up votes in the polls with a 6-0 loss to that team.

WALDENISM

I was never one to get worried about a team running up the score or not taking out their starters at some point. I never bought into that. I was taught as a young coach that you should take care of your team and let the other coach take care of his. Besides, if we want them not to run the score up, we need to do a better job of coaching our guys to prevent it. That's our fault... not theirs.

NICE SHOES, TERRY

As much as I hated the postgame handshake, I really enjoyed the quiet moments before the game when you have the opportunity to visit with the opposing coach. Afterward, there's people pushing and shoving and you're so emotional, and one of you is all bent up about losing. Before the game, a head coach doesn't have much to do. All the assistants have their guys warming up, so the head coaches always get together for a little chit-chat about nothing.

Sometimes you talk about how some other teams are doing, or how well one of their players is performing. If you want to know the truth, a lot of times you're just sort of sparring with him. You're both a little nervous and you both know what you've got to do that day. I enjoyed keeping it loose and having some fun, and after a while, coaches around the league learned that I might kid them a little bit when we met out there for our little unofficial conferences.

UCLA coach Terry Donahue and I were good friends and still are. One year we were at Pasadena to play them and out came Terry, wearing his regular coaching outfit, but with a pair of penny loafers on his feet. He looked like he was going someplace to pick up a cup of coffee. I looked at those shoes, but didn't say a word. We chit-chatted. I looked down at his shoes. We chit-chatted. I looked down at his shoes.

"All right, Jim, don't start with me," he said.

"No, no, Terry, those are great. What… are you planning on making short work of us and then gettin' out of Dodge in a hurry afterward?"

Right away, he started begging me not to tell the media that he was taking the game lightly because he showed up in penny loafers. "The manager forgot to get my coaching shoes out of the bag," he said. "You have no idea how badly I wanted to stay away from you today because I knew you were going to give me a hard time about it."

I couldn't help myself, having to add one more jab: "I bet you never coach in penny loafers when you're playing USC."

FRANK KUSH

My first year as head coach was a tough season, as we won only one conference game in 1978. But that win got the attention of our opponents that day, and helped a newcomer get a sense of how competitive the Pac-10 was going to be.

Arizona State came into Albi Stadium in Spokane that day to play its first game against a Pac-10 team as a Pac-10 member. ASU coach Frank Kush was excited about coming into the conference, and I'm sure he was drooling all over himself with the thought of opening up with a team they thought was maybe the worst in the league.

Well, Jack Thompson had a terrific day, and we clobbered the Sun Devils 51-26. Coach Kush told me that he'd never been so shocked. If we were the worst team in the league, and we could beat them this badly, man, they've got their work cut out for them.

He said he was so surprised that he was tempted to make his team practice in the parking lot right after the game. His team still finished in the top 20 that season, but he later told me that we gave the Sun Devils the best jolt they ever could have had.

CHAPTER 11

ON THE WAY UP

TALL COTTON

Coaching can be hard work, but let's not kid ourselves, there's much harder. I've seen harder work, real work. My grandparents knew hard work. My parents knew hard work. I'm proud of them, and I hope I learned from them. I grew up in Aberdeen, a small town in northern Mississippi, and we lived what would be considered a pretty bare existence. It was poor, but poor in the context of the times, during a period when a lot of people were poor. By the time World War II was over, I was seven or eight, and in the South in the mid-'40s, people didn't have many expectations. Religion was about all people had to hold on to.

My dad ran a service station and my mom worked in a garment factory; they worked hard and paid their taxes and were committed to the idea that their kids would get educations. My dad had an eighth-grade education and my mom finally graduated with a GED after having dropped out of school in the 10th grade.

What did I learn from those circumstances? I learned to say "Yes, sir" and "No, sir." I learned to go to church and be reverent. I was a rambunctious, wild horse of a kid, and did I get spanked? Man, oh, man. Did I need it? Yeah. I'll tell you, those "time-out" deals wouldn't have worked on me.

Until I was 15, I still had both grandparents on both sides, and I absolutely worshipped them. My mom's parents lived in Memphis, and when I went to visit them we'd go down to the rail yards and watch the steam locomotives. It was like something out of every kid's dream. Nothing could be more exciting for a young boy. My dad's parents lived on a farm about 15 miles from where I grew up. I'd go out there and Grandpa used to let me drive the mules and pick cotton, things you'd complain about if it was your job, but it was such great adventure for a kid.

Sometimes when Grandpa was plowing fields, Grandma would put on a big straw hat and we'd dig a can of worms, get two cane poles and go down to the creek and catch catfish. I was blessed to experience all that... all that fun, all that love.

My mother is still living; she still scolds me, too. If I picked up the phone and told her I was doing something she didn't approve of, she'd give me a three-minute dissertation on why I'm going to hell.

CHAW

I know, I know... it's gross. I've heard all about it. I used to get letters from people asking me how I could chew that icky tobacco on the sidelines. Television got me to stop it—at least on Saturdays. For a long time, we never had much TV exposure, so nobody cared about me chewin' a wad of Red Man on the sidelines. But after a while, when they'd broadcast

I know, the big lump of tobacco in my cheek looks stupid.
But I'd been chewin' since I was a little guy in Mississippi, and
it was a hard habit to break. One thing, though, it usually
caused everybody to give me a little space on the sidelines.
(Photo courtesy of Washington State University)

a game, they'd get those close-up shots of Jim Walden spitting, and that was pretty disgusting. It just was not fair that people had to watch that.

Players used to kid that you had to stay out of spitting radius of Coach Walden. And they said you had to be damned sure you didn't walk in front of him without him seeing you coming. Stopping liked to have killed me; I tried chewing gum but my jaws were so sore by the end of the game I could hardly open my mouth.

I guess I could blame it on my Southern heritage. I started chewing when I was 12, I think, maybe even before. It's just something you always did. You'd go out to play baseball and put a big chew in. You'd get in trouble if you went behind the barn and smoked a cigarette, but nobody down there cared if you chewed.

I was coaching for Bob Devaney at Nebraska when they put in their first AstroTurf surface. It was this beautiful green carpet and I was out there coaching one day… and chewing, of course. Coach Devaney came up to me and said: "Are you really spittin' on this beautiful new field we just put in for a quarter million dollars?" I told him the rain would wash it off, and besides, if we just paid a quarter million for a field and it couldn't stand up to a little tobacco juice, we've got big problems. He just walked away shaking his head… staying out of range.

I still chew when I'm out mowing the lawn or if I'm up at the lake, I'll still take a dip. And the answer is, yes, it tastes about like you'd think it does… pretty yucky.

THANK YOU, WYOMING

Going to the University of Wyoming was the best thing I could have done because it gave me the most important person in my life, my wife Janice. I could not ever, ever, have been given anyone I could love any more than Janice. I met her at Wyoming, and I also developed some wonderful friendships there. And in Bob Devaney, I played under a coach I could not have respected more. I could only hope that I've lived up to the standards he set as a coach and human being.

ACROSS THE BORDER

I was picked in the first round of the first draft the Denver Broncos ever had in the American Football League. Cleveland drafted me, too, but they just had a quarterback named Milt Plum take over for Otto Graham, and I didn't see much future there.

I think the Broncos wanted a local quarterback, and I was from Wyoming so I fit the description. But the franchise was a joke; they dressed in Quonset huts and didn't know from day to day where they were going to play. Going with them was tempting, because it was so close, but it wasn't much of an offer. The Broncos offered me $12,000 with a $5,000 signing bonus, and the B.C. Lions offered me $16,000 with the same signing bonus. So the kid from Mississippi decided he'd try to learn to speak Canadian.

Back then, there were only 13 teams in the NFL, so the level of competition in the CFL was pretty strong. Right off, I met a dear friend in Randy Duncan, an All-America quarterback from Iowa. What we discovered was that whichever one of us was quarterbacking, the fans always wanted the other guy.

The rule was that you could have only 12 Americans on the active list, so if I wasn't quarterbacking at the time, I had to play somewhere else. I played safety, which I didn't mind because I always had done that and it didn't bother me. I didn't have any great success, but I had a lot of fun up there.

SHOE SHINES AND DETERGENT

You get out there on the sidelines of the Apple Cup or a bowl game and fans imagine the life of a coach being this glamorous existence. And it is, it's wonderful. But almost nobody understands what it takes to get to that point. There were a lot of years of driving the bus, picking up the towels and lining the fields for high school teams.

Back when I coached high school kids, on Thursdays, I used to help our grounds man chalk the field. On Thursday nights, I'd shine everybody's shoes and polish their helmets so they'd look really sharp under the lights. That's part of what being a coach is at that level; it makes for a long, exhausting day, but you do everything you can to help those kids feel proud of themselves, and feel special about being on that field.

You learn a lot of valuable things that way, too. On Sundays, I'd work on my scouting reports at the laundromat between washing loads of dirty game uniforms. I did it so often, I knew every woman in town who didn't have her own washer and dryer.

There'd be 40 or 45 muddy uniforms that had to get cleaned, so I'd use those big front-loading washers. Pretty quickly you learn that you can't use a lot of a high-suds detergent like Tide with those big front-loaders because you'd get bubbles all over the place. I'd see some young wife come in there and start loading up the Tide on those front-loaders and I'd try to warn her. They'd be like: "Who is this guy?" But, don't look now, bubbles were soon flying everywhere. They just didn't want to listen to the football coach giving them advice about laundry soap.

You couldn't let your managers do the wash, either, unless it was maybe a senior who had been through it with you. Sure as shootin', they'll put the red jerseys in with the white pants and you'd be playing next Friday in all-pink uniforms.

I can't prove that going through all those things eventually makes you a better college coach. But I can testify that it makes you a more appreciative one.

RACE RELATIONS

People have asked me about growing up in Mississippi in the 1940s and '50s, and I try to tell them what it was like. I lived in a small town, half black and half white. It was a time of segregation, and a lot of us, as kids, didn't really understand or make judgments on it, because that's the way it was and we had nothing else to draw from.

Sometimes you can't realize what a thing is until you get away from it. I know that everybody in town traded with everybody else; that's how the economy worked. And while there was separation, there was never any on the playgrounds and play fields. All the kids played together, played sports, all the time. If there was a unifying element to the community, even at that time in Mississippi, it was sports.

BREAKING THE COLOR BARRIER

Those with a sense of history can imagine the atmosphere in Mississippi in 1966. Society was changing, and some notions of how things had been done were about to be seriously altered. Although Amory, Mississippi, where I was coaching at the time, was a very forward-thinking town, I knew I had reached a moment that had potential impact beyond our little region.

That fall, as I understood it, I was going to play the first black player on a traditional "white" school team in the history of Mississippi. I knew I needed to get out in front of this from the start, to be open, and let people know how this was going to go right up front.

I called a meeting of the parents and informed them that there were three young black athletes who were going to be playing on the team. I wanted them to know from me, before anybody started forming other ideas, how it was going to be handled. If this situation was against their beliefs of what was proper, I encouraged them to take their sons home that day and never say another word.

They could take them, but don't create a fuss, don't make this harder than it has to be. This is the direction things are going, I told them, and we don't have to have a problem with it. If you decide your son is going to stay, then I don't ever want to see or hear of another problem about race. I promised that if we handled it this way, I would do absolutely everything in my power to be fair to everybody on the team and make it work.

Not one player quit, and not one parent caused a problem. The downtown coffee-shop guys never raised an eyebrow. One of the three players, Doug Burdine, took the opening kickoff and ran it to midfield and, as far as I know, nobody ever said a negative word about it. I think that said volumes about the people of Amory, Mississippi.

About three years after he left high school, Doug Burdine was shot and killed in a honky-tonk bar.

CHAPTER 12

COUGAR COACHES

GEORGE, BOBO AND CHAPPY

For a time, the group of head coaches at Washington State included George Raveling, Bobo Brayton, John Chaplin and Jim Walden. I'll tell you what, we didn't win all the games in the world, but, man, the events were sure fun.

Maybe it's egotistical of me to include myself in that group, but I'm not sure there's many universities that had a foursome with such strong and different personalities. If nothing else, this was a Mt. Rushmore of quote-makers. In truth, three of the reasons I absolutely loved my time at Washington State were Raveling, Brayton and Chaplin. They were all there when I took over in '78, and they made me feel welcome and were always helpful.

There was the wit and charm of basketball coach George Raveling, the go-go-go personality of baseball coach Bobo Brayton, and the indescribable phenomenon that was track coach John Chaplin, who is like no one else you'll ever know in your life.

I learned a lot from George, just seeing him work a crowd, and dealing with some of the early issues of being a black head basketball coach in a small town like Pullman back in the '70s. He was just a joy.

Bobo came in one day and conned me into buying some box seats at the baseball park. They were nice, six seats on the third-base side, and I spent about a thousand bucks a season on them. But whenever I told Bobo I was going to come over for a game, he'd tell me, "Sorry, Jim, not today, I've got some important people sitting in there." For three years, I never got to sit in those seats.

John Chaplin was not only the track coach, but he was my NCAA rules compliance officer, too. John and I got along beautifully, and still do. John could chew me out over something, and I always sat there and took it because I knew it gave him so much pleasure. At the same time, he was so functional to have on your side because he knew what he was doing and he could sure get things done.

I have such total admiration for those guys and absolutely loved having the privilege of working with them.

THE COURT JESTER

As great a coach as George Raveling was, some of his best performances came off the court. He was a truly funny man with a lightning wit and the capacity to charmingly disarm any situation.

Remember, to be a black coach in rural Washington in the late '70s was to face a challenge. George had heard rumblings of discontent about the number of black players on his basketball team. As always, he defused the issue with humor. At Cougar gatherings, he used to say: "I know some of you are concerned, and I understand there's been some thought that we need some more white guys on our team. So, this year I went out and recruited Roosevelt White and Willie White."

Another time at a gathering, someone from the audience informed George that he had missed the latest episode of *Roots*, and wondered if the coach could fill him in.

Never missing a beat, George shot back: "Was that the one where I invented basketball?"

CHAPLIN'S SERMON

For a while, only one thing could slow down the great Henry Rono: A shouted threat by track coach John Chaplin.

Chaplin and Oregon coach Bill Dellinger were great friends, but John Chaplin was an Oregon fan's most hated rival. Those Oregon-Washington State dual track meets back then were Northwest treasures, and 15,000 fans would pack Hayward Field for them.

Without question, Henry Rono was the greatest athlete I ever saw. People talk about quarterbacks and running backs… I don't care, there was never a Cougar athlete like Henry Rono. For a time, he owned four world records in distance events. We used to reschedule our spring scrimmages if the Cougars had a track meet just so the players and staff would be done in time to go watch Rono run.

One year at Oregon, Rono was on pace to break one of his world records. Chaplin swore he'd never give those fans the pleasure of watching that kind of performance, so he ran down to where he could get Henry's attention as he came around a turn and started screaming: "Slow down, if you break the record here, I'll cut you from the team."

We asked John if he thought that would make the Oregon fans hate him. Hey, he said, "Who cares, they hate me already." That's how intense John Chaplin was.

GOLDEN RUEL

Part of what made Washington State so much fun was that we always had a staff filled with characters. One of the most energetic, imaginative coaches we ever had was Pat Ruel, whose actual given name was Golden Pat Ruel. Golden Ruel. He was just an unbelievable guy and an incredibly inventive coach.

Friday nights were our game-prep nights, and he'd give his offensive linemen their weekly tip sheets. The thing about his was that they were dressed up with cartoons he had drawn. He'd sometimes stay up all night on Thursday doing these things, and his players couldn't wait to get them because they were hilarious. It was such a unique approach, and he spent so much time on them, the players seem to give greater effort in absorbing the message. That's effective coaching.

Here's how goofy—and creative—Pat was. One winter he heard there was a Santa Claus at the mall over in Moscow, Idaho. He got his Cougar coaching attire on, got in line with all the little tykes, and sat down on Santa's lap. Here's this grown man in his coaching gear on Santa's lap. He got a bunch of these pictures made up and sent them off to recruits with the caption: "My Christmas wish for Santa is that you come to play at Washington State."

That guy never came up short; he was such a unique character you had no idea what he was going to come up with next.

Recruits and recruits' families just loved him, of course. And so did we; he helped make it fun to come to work.

One time I saw him in his office with about six Monopoly games spread out in front of him. He was taking that fake money out and putting it in piles. He'd stuff about $25,000 in an envelope with the message: "At Washington State, we don't cheat, but if I could, I'd pay this much for you." The players and parents were knocked out by it, it was such a different approach.

I know we signed guys who we never would have gotten were it not for Pat's creativity. One terrific prospect we almost got was a linebacker from the Bay Area who went to Cal and ended up in the NFL with the Chicago Bears... Ron Rivera. I don't think he'd have given us the time of day if it weren't for Pat's style. Rivera's folks loved Pat so much they were almost convinced that it would be better for him to come all the way up to Pullman than to sign with Cal, which would be so convenient for them in terms of getting to all his games. They almost cried when they had to tell Pat that Ron finally decided to go to Cal.

Sadly, Santa doesn't grant every coach's recruiting wish.

WALDENISM

I never agreed with the theory that you win with character not characters. I really felt you had to have both to make up a good team. It takes character to be successful, but you also can be a character while you're doing it. A lot of our coaches and players were real colorful and memorable characters over the years, and it made for a remarkable environment.

DEL WIGHT

We used to have a rookie day performance, and one of the all-time classic skits was performed by Erik Howard. These things were no-holds-barred affairs. You couldn't be outright nasty, but players could sure poke fun at their coach.

Erik nailed defensive line coach Del Wight perfectly. He came out dressed exactly how Del would, and he sat down, turned on a projector and started yelling with Del's distinctive gravelly voice. "Howard, get over there… Millard, you lazy S.O.B…" It was exactly like I was listening to Del Wight. We were doubled over laughing. But then he finished the film and turned on the lights and uttered the punch line: "Okay, get the players in here."

I almost couldn't breathe I was laughing so hard. See, Del used to sit in the room and watch film and scream at the players even when nobody else was in the room. Erik had picked up on it.

Del was kind of a cowboy from Wyoming and he dressed the part. One day he wore some fancy boots to a staff barbecue and one of the coaches asked him if they were Tony Lamas. "Llamas?" Del asked. "Nah, these are lizard skin."

"LONE STAR" DIETZ

Some folks like to kid me about being less than bashful in public. True enough, I enjoy the interplay and love meeting and mixing with the fans. I don't mind telling a story or two on occasion. But if you're looking for the most colorful Washington State coach of all time, the hands-down winner is

William "Lone Star" Dietz, who led the team to a January 1, 1916, win over Brown in the Rose Bowl.

From what I've read, Dietz used to walk the sidelines wearing a tuxedo jacket and top hat, smoking a cigar and heeling a Russian Wolfhound. Do you think that might make the SportsCenter highlights today? In some pictures, he's shown outfitted in full buckskins and a Native American chief's feathered head dress.

Dietz was half Oglala Sioux, and was a talented athlete, artist, actor and coach. He played at the famed Carlisle Indian School as a blocking back for Jim Thorpe. Dietz got into coaching with Carlisle's Glen "Pop" Warner, and then headed west to take over the young program at Washington State.

In 1915, behind Dietz's innovative defensive schemes, his team went 6-0 and was invited to play in the Pasadena Tournament of Roses East-West game. It wasn't even called the Rose Bowl yet. He only had 17 players, but when they hit Hollywood, Dietz got a job acting in a movie and his players were signed on as "extras." In their free time, they shut out Brown 14-0 to win the game.

As the story is told, Dietz bounced around, coaching all over the country, and died poor and alone in 1964 in Reading, Pennsylvania. Sad ending. When it comes to the history of Washington State football coaching, Dietz was hardly the lone star, but he was the first, and certainly the most colorful.

THE BABE

While Cougar historians are familiar with the efforts of O.E. "Babe" Hollingbery as Washington State's coach from 1926 through 1942, fewer might recall his close affiliation with the East-West Shrine game. Hollingbery initiated the

Coach Babe Hollingbery, here with Cougar great
Glen "Turk" Edwards, took the Cougars to the 1931
Rose Bowl. He also initiated the East-West Game.
(Photo courtesy of Washington State University)

game, and served as the coach on an annual basis. The East-West organizers, in fact, present a Hollingbery Award to those who show distinguished service to the game. I was honored to receive it myself after having played in the game, served as an assistant and head coach. Now I work for their organization. It's one of the most flattering awards I've received, and I felt it was an interesting connection that a Cougar coach would be honored with an award named after Coach Hollingbery.

Of course, that was hardly the lone claim to fame for Hollingbery, whose 1930 Cougar team went 9-0 and advanced to the Rose Bowl, where it was defeated, 24-0, by Alabama. That team, which was led by future College Football Hall of Fame inductees Mel Hein and Glen "Turk" Edwards, was Washington State's last bowl representative until we went to the Holiday Bowl in 1981.

JIM SWEENEY

You could never hold Jim Sweeney responsible for the revolving-door coaching situation at Washington State. He left after the '75 season, but he had been there eight years and had no control over what would happen in the next two years, when Jackie Sherrill and Warren Powers got the merry-go-round cranked up.

I got to know Jim afterward, and he's such a highly enthusiastic and energetic guy. I think he would tell you he wished he had done some things differently at Washington State. He told me that the last year, when he had a lead on Washington and lost the game, was his most heartbreaking thing. He was a coach with a gregarious personality, and I know he loves Washington State and I know he fought his share of tough battles there.

JACKIE SHERRILL

Jackie Sherrill came in and had a cup of coffee and left. I will give him credit, he compiled a great staff. Future Dallas Cowboys coach Dave Campo was on that staff, with some other really good coaches.

Dave told me one time that when Jackie left for Pittsburgh, he told Dave to stay by the phone because once he got settled in, he'd be calling him. Dave said about a year and a half later, when he was coaching at Weber State, he remembered that Jackie never did call him. Some of those guys are still waiting to hear from Jackie.

DENNIS ERICKSON

I knew that Dennis Erickson was taking over a group of talented kids after I left for Iowa State. We knew those '84 and '85 recruiting classes were going to be really special with Timm Rosenbach, Steve Broussard and so many other talented players.

When I left, I thought Dennis would get the job… I know I recommended him for it. I thought he could do some great

Dennis Erickson stayed only two seasons, but he did a great job, and when he left, he had the Cougars pointed in the right direction. (Photo courtesy of Washington State University)

things at Washington State. I think Dennis was a little over-whelmed his first year, as a lot of coaches can be when they change conferences and level of play. He later admitted that he was surprised by the speed of the athletes and the quality of the competition in the Pac-10.

When he was at Idaho, he and his staff used to come over and watch our practices on occasion, and our guys would go over there when we had some time. I think he probably looked at our guys and was sure he could win a lot of games with our talent. That's not a bad thing, but exactly how any competitive coach would feel.

They struggled that first year, but Dennis was an absolute quick work in progress as he turned it around in a hurry that next year, going 9-3. He saw in no uncertain terms what need-ed to be done, and that year they did it. Which I fully expect-ed he would.

Dennis came into town and did a nice job with the team. I think some people were mad he left so soon, but going to Miami wasn't a bad opportunity.

MIKE PRICE

Mike Price should be remembered by Cougar fans as a guy, along with his staff, who brought great dignity, respect, and winning on a consistent basis to Washington State. He is a coach who had fun doing it and made sure his players had fun along the way, too. He did for Washington State what coach-ing should be all about, taking a team to the highest pinnacle and enjoying the trip. He did a marvelous job.

We were on Warren Powers's staff together in 1977. He went with Powers to Missouri and our paths didn't cross much after that. The one thing I remember about Mike as an assistant, and I've kidded him about this, is that he's the only coach I ever knew who missed practice because he was sick. You know, if you breathe, you coach. That's kind of the unwritten rule. Sometimes you'd feel like you'd have to get healthier just to die, but you got out there and coached.

One day we sat down for our coaches meeting and Price wasn't there. The secretary came in and said Mike just called, he's real sick and he's going to stay home. We all kind of looked at each other. The next day was the same. I think at that point we all told Warren that Price has got to get his ass in here. And he did. I've ribbed him about it; in 31 years of coaching, with all those guys on all those staffs, I've never seen a coach miss a practice because he was sick. Only Mike Price.

He did a phenomenal job at Washington State... except for a couple sick days.

UNHEARD ADVICE

I'll be honest, I prayed that Mike Price wouldn't take that job at Alabama. My thinking was, you've spent 14 years at Washington State, why not spend six more? But Mike wanted to take that challenge and that's understandable. I know he thought he was ready for what he was getting into, but he wasn't.

Heck, I wasn't even prepared for the increased scrutiny when I went to Iowa State, and that's nothing like Alabama. Every Tuesday there were five television stations and a hundred tape recorders up on that desk. And that's not even considering talk radio. I was overwhelmed, and I'm not a good person in some of those situations, because I always speak my mind, which could get me in trouble.

At Washington State, the only hint of that you get is Apple Cup week, and even that isn't nearly as much pressure as it is every single day at Alabama. Down there, the three main religions are Baptist, Methodist and Football. They take it that seriously.

I wanted to warn Mike about this. I grew up in the South; my sister lives in Tuscaloosa, my brother-in-law was assistant pastor of the First Baptist Church of Tuscaloosa. I truly know what the culture is there. I knew that you could not go into a bar in that state without the entire state knowing about it. I knew that there's a good-ol' boy system down there that will absolutely eat you alive if you don't understand it.

Mike's a grown man, and the fallout from the trouble he got in down there will die down and he will be be loved, as well he should be, by the Cougar family. I just wanted to warn him about all of these potential problems. I called him when he got the job and left a message telling him that I would welcome the opportunity to tell him about all these things, that maybe the advice would be helpful in dealing with it. At least it might put him on the lookout for the kinds of things that could happen.

But he chose not to call back.

BILL DOBA

It was a stroke of genius hiring Bill Doba; I have loved this guy since I knew who he was. Mike Price has had so many good assistants, but in 14 years, I don't know if there's ever been a more solid coach than Bill Doba. I have to compliment Jim Sterk, in the highest fashion, as a young athletic director. He was smart enough to hire Bill Doba for football and Dick

Bennett for basketball, and not be influenced by age or any other factor. He just hired the best guys and it was the perfect thing to do.

The thing about Bill is that he's such a top-notch guy and the players love and respect him. Maybe the best thing is that when you ask him a question, you get a straight answer. You know he's telling you the best he knows how. And he's got a nice sense of humor that he's kind of sneaky with.

I also think he assembled one of the best staffs that Washington State has ever had. These guys are so knowledgeable, his first staff had five of them who were former Cougars: Ken Greene, Mike Levenseller, Mike Walker, George Yarno and Timm Rosenbach. You know that former Cougars are going to lay it on the line.

Washington State was put in terrific hands with Bill Doba.

WALDENISM

Nothing brings me more satisfaction than the success the Cougars are having. I'm always smiling about it. I call up my old assistants and we talk about how good it is. It's heartwarming to me because I'm one of those who knows from whence they came.

CHAPTER 13

RECORDS AND HEARTBREAK

MARK RYPIEN

I occasionally got impatient with quarterback Mark Rypien, but I was always cautious not to get the hook out and pull him out of the game too soon, because he could heat up like nobody you've ever seen. Mark was like that old nursery rhyme, when he was bad, he could be pretty bad. But when he was good, when he got hot, it was amazing the things he could do.

You weren't always sure, even from series to series, what he was going to give you. But he could turn it around in a hurry. One of the great examples was against Cal at home in 1985, when we were losing 19-0 through three quarters. He lit up, and in less than nine minutes, he must have thrown for 250 yards and completed maybe 15 of his next 16 passes. We scored 20 points in eight minutes and he was the best quarterback on Planet Earth.

On the sidelines in games when he struggled, I used to say to him: "Mark, do you think you're going to be able to play a little bit better at any point today? Any time you want to start on that, you have my permission." He's not a guy you had to jump on, and you wanted to be patient with him because he was such an unbelievable athlete.

The one year he broke his collarbone and was redshirting was hard on him. One Sunday, rumor got to us that Mark was going to go home, maybe to transfer someplace else and switch to baseball. He could have done that because of the talent he had. At the time, Ricky Turner was playing well, and I think Mark was worried that Ricky was going to be the future at quarterback. The other problem was that he felt that nobody was spending much time with him. That's true, there's almost nothing so lonely as a football player who is injured and isn't playing. The coaches are so busy dealing with the healthy players that there just isn't much time to pay attention to those who are hurt. Coaches don't love you less, they just can't afford to spend a lot of time telling you about it.

So, I drove up to Spokane and sat down with Mark and his parents and had a long chat with him and his dad, Bob. His father was a wonderful guy who loved his kids and lived for them. He had a tremendous impact on his sons. I think Bob was feeling that Mark had made a mistake coming to Washington State.

They just needed reassuring. I told them how things worked in this type of situation. There had been a lot of unreasonable expectations on Mark; he was one of the most highly recruited athletes in the state of Washington, and he was hurt and inactive, and that was probably another kind of pressure on him. In less than an hour, it was taken care of and I was driving back to Pullman. He was back in school Monday morning, and I don't think he even missed a class.

Cougar baseball coach Bobo Brayton called me up and said, "Hey, Jim, if he wants to quit football to play baseball, try to get him to stay here and play for me." Thanks for the support, Bobo.

One of our all-time great recruits, Mark Rypien could match any quarterback in the country when he was hot. We like to think some of the skills that helped him become a Super Bowl MVP were learned at Washington State. (Photo courtesy of Washington State University)

Mark had some wonderful games for us and was a terrific, humble guy. And he still is. I was so disappointed when he wasn't drafted until the sixth round. But I knew the Washington Redskins were going to get one great bargain with that pick.

SUPER PREPARATION

After Mark Rypien had gone off to the NFL, I got a call from Redskins coach Joe Gibbs. I figured he wanted to talk about one of our current athletes, but he just wanted to compliment us on the job we did of teaching Mark the mechanics of sprint-out passing. He said he was shocked by Mark's ability to throw on the run, and it was going to be a real benefit to him playing in Gibbs's offense.

Some people think maybe Mark didn't win enough games when he was at Washington State, but getting him as a recruit was huge for us, and he gave us many terrific performances. It was good to hear from Coach Gibbs that having been at Washington State was helpful for Mark's career in the NFL, too.

Of course, he went on to be the MVP of Super Bowl XXVI and have a marvelous career.

WORST LOSS...
NON-APPLE CUP DIVISION

It had been 26 years since a Washington State football team had defeated UCLA or USC in Los Angeles. But with time running down, the game tied and us facing a reasonable 44-yard field goal by reliable kicker John Traut, it definitely felt as if we were going to put another bad streak behind us in 1984.

They had us down early, but with Rueben Mayes rushing for 156 yards and Mark Rypien getting hot passing, we came back to tie it. With about a minute and a half left, we started going through possible scenarios. At worst, we miss the kick and go home with a 24-24 tie. Not bad. UCLA was a team that would finish 9-3 and ranked ninth in the country. At best, though, John boots it through and we get the first win in L.A. for what seems like 100 years.

Unfortunately, I never imagined there could be a third scenario, and that was what made this simply the most difficult, gut-wrenching, jerk-your-heart-out loss we ever went through. People immediately blamed the botched field goal on snapper Bill Williams. But the problem that started it all occurred on Thursday that week. Pili Tutuvanu was our snapper, but on Thursday afternoon, when we were just working out in light pads and shorts, some kid whipped around on a play and clobbered Pili in the side of the leg and blew out his knee.

That left Billy Williams as our snapper, facing a job he'd never really done before. But he was all we had left and he'd give it his best. When the crucial moment came in Pasadena, as he went to snap the ball, he somehow had one of his thumbs bang up against his face mask, and the ball went about four feet before it hit the ground and started hopping wildly. Ed Blount was the holder, but there was no way he could get hold of it.

Now, everybody was running around back there trying to pick it up. Guys dove on it, and it squirted farther, and somebody else grabbed at it and it went farther. By the time UCLA recovered it, it was all the way back near the 50. With no timeouts, UCLA quarterback Steve Bono got them in position for a 47-yard field goal for John Lee, who was probably the best kicker in the nation that year. He made it.

It was strange, we had some screwy things happen in games against UCLA, like the '81 game at home when we were beating the Bruins and just trying to run out the clock in the last minute. Timmy Harris fumbled the ball on a simple dive up the middle and they came back, threw two passes and kicked the field goal to leave us tied at 17-17. Had we won that game, we'd have had the Rose Bowl berth locked up before we played Washington, a game we lost to cost us the conference title.

So, maybe I should have envisioned what happened in '84. I couldn't be down on Billy Williams, though. He didn't mean to do it. The guy I needed to be mad at was the kid who hurt Pili Tutuvanu on Thursday. He was the real culprit.

RUEBEN MAYES

The tapes we got of this Canadian running back looked liked they'd been taken from the back of a pickup truck. Through the scratches and bad lighting, about all we could see is a kid who kept running for touchdowns every time he touched the ball. We couldn't tell much about the level of competition; all we could see was one player who was far, far better than anybody else out there.

One of our assistants, Bob Padilla, used to go up and serve as a guest coach for old Cougar receiver Hugh Campbell, who was coaching the Edmonton Eskimos. Bob got to know a high school coach who sent down films of a back from North

Battleford, Saskatchewan, named Rueben Mayes. We tried to research him the best we could, but high-school football in Canada is pretty sketchy. All we could come up with was a sprint time he ran in a meet when he was 14… and it proved he was plenty fast.

What the heck, on the coach's advice, we invited him down for a visit, and we discovered the nicest young man, a wonderful guy with bright eyes and nothing but eagerness for an opportunity to play college football. He said, "Coach, I don't know how much I lack in some areas, but I promise you I'll make up for anything with hard work."

I told Bob that I was ready to give this kid a scholarship just for his manners. Even though we didn't have much to go on—a coach's recommendation, a scratchy film and an old track time—we knew we weren't going to find a better kid.

At the same time, we were recruiting a back out of Montana, Kerry Porter. And he was like a clone, another great kid. The two of them became the best of friends and were just a joy to coach. You'd never see two kids laugh and have so much fun, even while they were running 40-yard sprints. They loved to play, they loved to practice and they loved being out there at the same time. There was never one hint of jealousy and never a thought of, "Oh, I could get more carries if the other guy weren't here." To get two such great and unselfish players at the same time was unbelievable.

Kerry had a 1,000-yard rushing season in 1983, and Rueben came back with the blockbuster the next year (1,632 yards). Rueben went on to have a wonderful career in the NFL, and I'll have to say that the best part of it is that he hasn't changed a bit from the first time we sat down and talked. He's still the same pleasant, respectful, tremendous person he was all those years ago.

On this 1984 Saturday at Oregon's Autzen Stadium, Rueben Mayes ran past all the great running backs in college football history. Repeatedly shaking loose on draw play after draw play, Rueben picked up 357 rushing yards. What we loved about Rueben was that he was as fine a man as he was a running back. (Photo courtesy of Washington State University)

RUEBEN'S 357 MAGNUM

Rueben Mayes's biggest day, of course, was October 27, 1984, at Oregon's Autzen Stadium when he broke the NCAA single-game rushing record with 357 yards on 39 carries. I'll tell you this, we needed every single one of those yards, too, because Oregon was scoring about as fast as we were.

He must have gained about 200 yards on the 69 Draw play, which we may have run 25 times that day. They knew it was coming; they just couldn't stop it. The next time I saw Oregon coach Rich Brooks, he came up to me and acted like he was going to choke me. He said he was never more embarrassed in a game. "Do you know what it's like to have 40,000 people in the stands screaming 'Watch the drawwwwwwww!'," he said. "We tried everything we knew how to stop that and couldn't do it. Finally, I was yelling, 'Watch the drawwww!' along with them."

Because the game was so close, Rueben stayed on the field and we kept feeding him the ball. If it had been a runaway, he never would have had the chance to get into the record book. We finally won 50-41. We didn't keep Rueben in the game to get the record; we kept him in the game so we could win.

RELATIVE HUMILITY

A lot of players truly believe they're much better than they really are. At least a couple I had never really wanted to believe they were as good as they truly were. Dan Lynch and Kirk

Samuelson, both seniors in 1984, never understood they were as talented a pair of guards as I ever had. They were both real bright and wonderful guys, too, and few were more humble.

Dan finally may have gotten the feeling how dominating he could be his senior year when he made First-Team All-America. He was the best football player I ever coached who did not play in the National Football League. He just didn't have the bulk, but he was so smart and talented that he was a great college guard.

Kirk, on the other side, took even more convincing. As late as his senior year, he came in and said he was considering quitting because he didn't think he was good enough and wasn't helping the team. He meant it; he could not see the ability he had. I said, "Kirk, what part of this don't you understand? You started 11 games for us last year, you're our starting guard. We need you."

Some kids have problems with cockiness or arrogance. These two guys were the opposite. They were terrific players who always needed pep talks to be reminded of how valuable they were to our team.

APPLE CUP '84: HEARTBREAK

The pain of the '84 Apple Cup lives on not so much because of the 38-29 loss in a game we had under control, but in the way it branded one of my players as a scapegoat. It was unfair, it was incorrect, and a talented player ended up taking the blame for one of the worst examples of officiating I've ever seen.

We were kicking the daylights out of UW; Mark Rypien was really cookin', the crowd was really into it, and it felt like we were fixin' to stone them. We were up 26-16 and had stopped them on a third and three in their territory. It looked like we were going to get the ball back again and ride the momentum to a big win.

But linebacker Rico Tipton and their tight end got locked up a little bit on that play. You've seen this a thousand times, when two guys will come up and both be squared off a little bit. But they called us for unnecessary roughness and gave them 15 yards and a first down. It not only upset everybody, it cost us the momentum that we never got back. Give Washington credit, the Huskies did a nice job with the opportunity.

It was a sucker call and it was totally unnecessary. It was one of the all-time bad calls you should never see in a rivalry game. That official didn't understand the tempo of the game. You could eject both of them if you want. But don't call it on my guy when there's two of them locked up like that. I have no idea how somebody couldn't see their guy being involved, too. As usual, they did a great job of catching the retaliation.

Washington went on to an Orange Bowl win over Oklahoma to finish 11-1. We stayed home. It should have been three straight wins for us over the Huskies. What that could have done to the momentum of our program we'll never know.

And the world—wrongly—blamed Rico Tipton. That call gave Rico a burden he never should have to carry. He was a tremendous player who really did nothing wrong, and I've been upset that so many people want to remember his name in infamy. It was unfair and he didn't deserve it.

INFLATED IMAGE

One of our kids was just trying to have a little fun during Apple Cup week practices, but it probably didn't do us much good when game time rolled around. We assigned a scout team guy the job of portraying Washington's star running back Jacque Robinson in practice. Jacque was a great back, but it could not be said that he was one of those slender scatback types. He had, let's say, a low center of gravity.

I can't remember who it was, but that week our Jacque impersonator came onto the field with some foam rubber shoved down the back of his pants and the front of his jersey to make him look pretty tubby. Kids are always doing something to try to crack up their buddies; there's no group with a sicker sense of humor than what football players show toward each other.

I had nothing to do with this, of course, but I laughed along with everybody else. I was never against having a little fun, and I didn't think it was being particularly disrespectful. I'm not sure how it got to Don James or Jacque, but it did.

Of course, Jacque was slender enough to rush for 160 yards and three touchdowns. The joke was on us.

WALDENISM

I never cared much about the "bulletin board" fears that a lot of coaches have. I used to tell the players to not use bad language and not to directly point a finger at anybody. But if

you're asked a question, say what you believe and let your con-
science be your guide. And, of course, be prepared to back it
up.

RYPIEN IN STITCHES

No coach appreciates distracting calamities on the week of
the rivalry game, especially when they involve the starting
quarterback. Early in Apple Cup week 1984, word came to us
that Mark Rypien needed 15 stitches to close a cut on his hand
that he received when he "broke a water glass." My immediate
thought was: "Water glass, hmmm, yeah."

I asked him if he thought he could play and he said he was
sure he could. So he wore a glove all week and never missed a
snap. And he played pretty darn well in the game.

I didn't pursue the cause of the cut because I didn't think
there was reason to. Mostly, when a guy tells you something,
you believe him unless you have reports to the contrary. As far
as I knew, I had no reason not to believe him. He's never elab-
orated to me what happened beyond that. Do I believe the
story? Hhhmmmm, I'd give you 50-50.

CHAPTER 14

NOISE AND APOLOGIES

THE VOICE OF THE FEW

While I would like to say that I was pretty good at remaining under control on the sidelines, I concede that the limits of my patience occasionally were tested by officials. Once, it was for an absolutely ridiculous reason.

For a while, crowd noise was an issue that officials would try to administrate by charging the home team a delay-of-game penalty, or by giving the visitor a free timeout. But that depended on the official and the site, of course. We used to have a tough time at Arizona State in Tempe. Especially before they had pro football down there, the fans were extremely loyal and vocal at Sun Devil Stadium, which held about 75,000. We dealt with that every year we went down there, but we never got a break, never a timeout, never a penalty against them.

About the middle of the 1985 season, we had just lost a tough 31-30 game to UCLA at home in front of almost a full house. As it used to go a lot of the times when we lost, most of the people didn't come back the next week. When Arizona

State showed up in Pullman, we had an announced attendance of only 14,875.

But it was a close ball game, and when it looked like they were driving for a touchdown, our fans really got into it, trying to help us out. I was so proud of our little 14,000, they were beating their feet on those metal bleachers and screaming, and I was pretty amazed myself how much of a ruckus they were raising.

Their quarterback, Jeff Van Raaphorst, backed away from center and looked at the referee, who called timeout and came running over to me. I started screaming... what the heck is going on? He said, "Coach, if the crowd keeps this up, I'll have to assess you a timeout."

I couldn't believe it. "Look, I don't want to embarrass you, so let's make it look like we're just talking. I want you to look over my shoulder into the stands and you tell me how many people you see up there." He looked up kind of shyly and saw that it was maybe half-full.

I said, "Okay, let's you and me kind of work our way around so you can look over my shoulder this other way, and you tell me how many people you see under the press box. What, maybe half-full?"

He nodded. "How 'bout in the end zones? Empty, right?" He nodded. "Now, why is it that they get a timeout when we've got less than 20,000 people here, and I go down there all the time in front of 75,000 and nobody ever gives me a timeout?"

He looked me right in the face and said: "Coach, I owe you an apology." He whirled right around, ran back out there and told that quarterback to get under center immediately and play football.

The fans had no idea what we were doing, waltzing around down there looking up into the stands, but I made my point. The beautiful thing was that on the next play, with the fans screaming their lungs out, the quarterback fumbled the exchange and we got the ball back.

They won, 21-16, but our 14,875 Cougar fans proved they could be a match for 75,000 Sun Devils.

WALDENISM

I don't think there's 10 percent of the officiating crews in the country that understand the pass interference rule. When I coached, the pass interference penalty was enacted at the point of the foul. That meant you could get tagged for 35 yards on a deep ball for what might be an iffy judgment call. All the coaches who had to deal with that awful penalty should be sent money every year as a refund for having to work under that brutal rule. It took years off our lives.

ERIK HOWARD

Erik Howard could bench press almost 400 pounds the day he got to Washington State, and he only got stronger. He was the strongest athlete we ever had. One of the pro scouts told me about a strength test they used to evaluate prospects. They put 225 pounds on the bar to see how many bench-press reps you could pound out.

Before Erik got down on the bench, he had only one question: "What's the record?"

The scout told him it's, oh, 45, I think. Eric nodded, laid down, and, man, the iron started flying. He got to 50, put the weights down, and said: "There, that ought to give them something to shoot for for a while."

MILFORD HODGE

I don't know if we've had a bigger success and a better feel-good story than Milford Hodge. We took him out of San Francisco and we had to really fight to get him in school; he got in by the narrowest of margins. When he showed up for fall camp, he was easily 20 pounds heavier than when we recruited him. He was so out of shape he almost couldn't run 100 yards. And his first semester, he struggled so badly that he almost flunked out.

But from that point, I've never seen a more dedicated man. On his own, he went in to our weight training people and came up with a program to get him in shape. Then he started catching on to what it was going to take to get his education. He was absolutely vigilant and unbelievably motivated.

His athleticism and his academics improved every year because of his hard work. We've had guys overcome bad educational backgrounds, but very few accomplished more than Milford Hodge. Now, he's an academic counselor with a master's degree at Washington State. He is one of our real success stories who make us so proud.

MY APOLOGIES

I'm still sick about the 1985 season. It was my worst job of coaching because there was no excuse for us not being better

Milford Hodge (79) was not only a fabulous defensive lineman, he was a man with uncommon determination. After coming to WSU in poor condition and unprepared to be a successful student, he worked hard enough to get himself into the NFL and earn a graduate degree. (Photo courtesy of Washington State University)

than 4-7. That was the RPM season (Mark Rypien, Kerry Porter, Rueben Mayes), and the way it turned out was not their fault; it was mine. Nothing the players did disappointed me. But almost everything I did that year disappointed me.

First, we scheduled ourselves out of contention. I allowed the Pac-10 to commit an unpardonable sin, scheduling us against Oregon, Cal and Arizona to start the season. That's three conference games in a row... have you ever heard of a conference doing such a thing to a team?

We lost to Oregon by three, beat Cal and then lost to Arizona 12-7... and we were out of the Rose Bowl race by September 14. When you're a Pac-10 team, there's nothing that keeps your hopes alive as much as being in the Rose Bowl race. After we started 1-2, we lost the team a little bit. I think I allowed them to realize that all hope was gone, and we didn't coach with sufficient urgency. Just because we lost two conference games didn't mean we couldn't come back and have a great season.

I have to apologize to that group. They know I love them, but I truly disappointed myself, and for that I owe them a huge apology.

APPLE CUP '85: ENJOYABLE

The schedule had been absurd, and we allowed it to turn this into a tremendously poor season. But there is nothing of greater salvation in a situation like that than a rivalry game. What we were left with was a chance to beat Washington and hope that would smooth out some of the wrinkles we'd developed during a disappointing season.

So, we dominated... until the last minute. It was 25 degrees at kickoff, with a biting wind coming off Lake

Washington. Mark Rypien threw three touchdown passes, Rueben Mayes rushed for 167 yards, and the defense was led by a big game by Erik Howard. But with time running out, they got back into it in a hurry. Quarterback Chris Chandler threw a little drag route across the middle to Mo Hill, and one of our guys held onto his jersey for about five yards before Hill broke away and ran in for a 50-yard touchdown.

The game that seemed so well in hand quickly started looking like a potential loss. That score cut our lead to 21-20. Bless his heart, Washington coach Don James decided to go for the two-point conversion. He later explained: "I didn't think there was any need to come in here and tie the game." There were no overtimes in those days, and nobody ever wanted to go for a tie in a rivalry game. Thank heavens.

The Huskies later said they were expecting some manner of zone coverage on the conversion attempt, but we went with man coverage and blitzed free safety Kevin Thomasson. It worked perfectly, as Kevin broke through and got his hands in Chandler's face to force him to release it early in the direction of Mo Hill. The ball was uncatchable, and we registered our third win over UW in four seasons.

I felt so happy for Mark Rypien; I knew how badly he wanted to beat them as the starting quarterback. Our three wins in four seasons against UW was an almost unbelievable stretch considering that run of eight straight losses the Cougars had been through. And I'd argue that the '85 win should have made it four Apple Cups in a row going our way if we hadn't suffered the late collapse in the '84 game.

CHAPTER 15

RIVALS TO THE CORE

THE DAWGFATHER

Some fans get so involved in our football rivalries that they almost expect us to hate our sworn rivals. But I can tell you honestly that I've never had anything but the greatest respect and admiration for former Washington coach Don James. Which doesn't mean I didn't do absolutely everything in my power to beat him every year.

I laughed when Don called himself a 2,000-word underdog to me. But, face it, he was. And I don't think he minded it. I always thought that head football coaches in the same state should be like boxers: They'll say things to stimulate the gate, they'll go for 15 rounds trying to knock each other's face off, but when it's over, you'll see two guys who truly do respect each other. They understand the battle and can step back and say that they did it with dignity and they're still friends.

That's the way it was with Don and me, and his wife, Carol, and my wife, Janice. The late Michigan State coach

Duffy Daugherty used to have us speak at his clinic and then he'd pay us with fabulous golf outings in the summer, to Ireland, Hong Kong, Spain, Hawaii, Bangkok. It was a wonderful thing, and Don and Carol and Janice and I always took these trips.

It's pretty clear that Don and I were opposites—introvert and extrovert—but he has a lot better sense of humor than people realize. The truth of it is, his wife, Carol, is more like me, and my wife, Janice, is more like Don. Maybe that's why we liked each other's company so much. We certainly were able to get above and beyond the rivalry on the field.

Make no bones about it, nobody liked living with losing to the other one. In some of those games, Washington had more to lose than we did, but I want you to know that, flat out, there's never a day in my life when losing to Washington didn't hurt me as much as losing to us hurt him. When he says how much it killed him to lose to Washington State, believe me, I didn't go dancing on the five nights after he whupped me. Don James and Jim Walden had one thing in coming: Losing to each other was never an option.

DON'S INTEGRITY

When I heard somebody accuse Don James of not being in control of his program, it absolutely broke my heart. There's no more bogus thing that could happen to a coach than the situation that happened to Don James at Washington. Don James was one of the five best coaches to ever coach this game in its history. When Don resigned, I told him how much I hated it, and how much I appreciated his professionalism. I was convinced that Washington was the big-time loser in that deal, and I told him that. I still feel that way.

You see a person's true character only when it's being tested. I can give you an example that few people know about that shows the strength and character of Don James.

Maybe as early as 1980, the Pac-10 Conference coaches had a meeting where we decided it wouldn't be good for any of us to be going around accusing each other of recruiting illegalities or irregularities. We had enough trouble protecting ourselves from schools on the outside that we should try, as best we could, to police ourselves.

If somebody had a problem, we were to pick up the phone, share the facts as we knew them, and if our investigations proved they were true, then that team would voluntarily drop out of recruiting that kid and we'd go from there.

All the time we were there, we only had one episode, and it involved a Washington assistant telling a recruit that it was okay at UW to sell books at the end of a semester and keep the money to help pay for the holiday trip home. That's not right, in fact, it's illegal as hell. I called Don and told him what I'd heard. Don, as professional as any man you'll ever deal with, said he'd look into it, handle it, and get right back to me. Within 30 minutes, the phone rang and Don said that the information was correct, UW had already informed the player that they were no longer recruiting him, and the assistant was warned that if any further complaints arose, he'd be immediately dismissed.

Just like that, it was taken care of. I didn't expect anything less because that's the way Don is. In all our years, we never got a complaint, so I think that that validates the way my coaches were doing things. And that also verifies, in no uncertain terms, Don James's commitment to doing things right.

IN THE DAWGHOUSE

Even as a devout Cougar, I take no delight in seeing the Huskies suffer. They've been through some troubles over there. And, frankly, some of it they've earned. I'd say, in a large part, they've gotten what they deserved.

If you look at history, when universities don't stand behind somebody who deserves administrative backing, it sets in motion a course of events that can turn out very badly. When they didn't support Don James when the Pac-10 was levying sanctions, they turned their backs on the most honest and hard-working coach they could ever have. The alumni were upset by that, they lost a certain amount of loyalty, and I think it was an absolute flagrant display of abandoning a person who gave so much to that university. How can something like that create a positive environment?

I think they should have said to the Pac-10: "Sure, give us whatever sanctions you want, but we stand behind Don James 100 percent, and everyone has to know that he is our man and we support him." Had they done that, I think they might have been able to keep him, and I believe that everything negative that has happened since would have been different. I can promise you they would have never gone through some of the coaching problems they had.

I liked Don's replacement, Jim Lambright, but I think he used bad judgment when he tried to disassociate himself from Don James. It seemed to me a poor idea to separate yourself from somebody the fans loved so much.

And so they went through the sanctions, they went through Jim Lambright's firing, and they went through the embarrassment that was Rick Neuheisel. I hope former athletic director Barbara Hedges doesn't get mad at me about this, but that's never stopped me before. It's just my opinion, but they made some dumb decisions in their handling of Don James, and they've been paying for it ever since.

RICK NEUHEISEL

I've been asked about the reputation of former Husky coach Rick Neuheisel, and I have to assume they didn't call him "Slick Rick" for nothing. I know that among coaches, even before he went to Washington, he wasn't the most well thought of guy, because he was always trying to push the envelope, trying to stretch or bend the rules.

He took the NCAA rule book and thought he could manipulate it like a defense lawyer in court. And you can't do that. People said he's trying to do ingenious things, but there's nothing left to be ingenious about in the rule book that isn't cheating. If you try something "ingenious," it's probably illegal. Like that story about him being across the street from a recruit and calling him on his cell phone while the kid is looking out the window. At a time when you're not supposed to have direct contact with a recruit, that's cheating. He can say, "Oh, I wasn't in his living room," but that's still eyeball to eyeball. That's not ingenious, that's cheating.

I think Rick kept trying to play with the rules, and I can tell you, other coaches don't appreciate that.

GILBY

I sure hope Washington football fans are smart enough to not hold the early struggles he had to face against coach Keith Gilbertson. That's not fair to him. This guy took over as head coach so late that it was impossible, given all the turmoil surrounding the program, to put together a strong first season.

I like Keith; I've known him since he was an assistant over at Idaho, and I've always had great respect for him. I've always thought of him as a very tenacious coach with a great coordinator's brain. He's one of the few coaches I ever thought was intelligent enough to coach the offensive line and be a coordinator, too.

There's no bigger job on a staff than the offensive line. That's where there's the most going on. He always has to deal with having the kitchen sink thrown at him. That takes an enormous amount of time. Keith was one of the rare guys who could do that and coordinate an offense at the same time. That's remarkable.

Keith is his own man, and he'll leave his own mark at Washington. I think he learned lessons as a head coach at California and Idaho that will help him at UW. Just don't evaluate his potential as a coach on the tough circumstances he faced in taking over a damaged program from Rick Neuheisel.

WALDENISM

There's fewer bad things going on in coaching today than 40 years ago. By far. There's better rules, better policing, and the biggest thing is there's more money at stake, which means there's more to lose by cheating. When you were making $13,000 a year, even if you got caught, you could pick up and go make that much at a car dealership. And there's no alumni you had to satisfy when you're selling Chevys.

CHAPTER 16

STRATEGY AND PHILOSOPHIES

TWELVE ANGRY MEN

I wasn't big on having a lot of rules, and I didn't enjoy screaming and hollering. But my coaches knew that I had one sacred commandment that would cause me to get very, very serious: If you're responsible for us getting a penalty for having 12 men on the field, I'm gonna fire you. I hated that penalty that much.

There's no reason for being out of control to that degree. I have never seen any time that penalty was called that it wasn't a classic mistake that cost you a possession and maybe even the game. It's the worst mistake in football. I'll tell you what, you've never seen so many coaches doing so much head-counting in a game as my assistants did on our sideline.

Now, things happen you can't control. A time or two every season some player would get his bell rung, but you wouldn't know it. All of a sudden, with no warning, some kid would go running onto the field before you can even see him. He'll just be goofy, and whatever is going on in his idle brain tells him it's time to go play. The other case is when you get a defensive back or linebacker hurt. These are guys who might be on three or four special teams, and they could have three or four different guys as backups on those units. That gets confusing.

So, did I ever have to fire anybody? No. We got called for the penalty only one time at Washington State, and it wasn't a coach's fault. A kid got hurt, came out, and was replaced. The original starter got better and rushed back out there, but his replacement didn't know that he was well again. We couldn't get a time out in time and we were penalized.

So, as it turned out, it was a player's fault. And I couldn't fire a player because, man, we just didn't have enough of them.

RUMP-TURN OPTION

We had a series of plays we called the Rump-Turn Option. Why call it that? To be honest, I can't remember. It required the backfield guys to take a step, turn their butts to the line of scrimmage, spin around and get out to the corner. The reason for the turn was because it froze the linebackers and it gave us time to pull a guard and get him out in front of the play. The synchronization of it was crucial.

I later found out that the women among our fans liked it because it looked so choreographed, with the three guys making a full spin in unison. You know, I agreed; I watched it on film and it was kind of pretty.

TWENTY-NINE REVERSE

We didn't run a lot of trick plays, but we had a reverse that was really one of the most dreaded in the country because we ran it differently than most teams. And, man, it was deadly. Not to get too technical, but 98 percent of the time teams run the wingback reversing to the split-end side. We ran the split end back to the flanker side off our counter-dive option.

The blocking was the same as our normal 29 option, but when the quarterback went to toss it to the pitch-back, the split end was coming back around to take the pitch the other way. Arizona and USC coach Larry Smith told me it was the most-hated play he ever faced. They even named it "That ?!#%*& Reverse."

What made it work was the need for defenses to have their people get over to defend all your options. We made a ton of yards on that thing; I'll bet we averaged about 15 yards a play, and it won us a lot of ball games. Really, we came up with it to protect our option. If defenses know they have to stay home because the reverse might be coming back at them, that slows down their pursuit. And even if we ended up losing two yards on the play, it helped us pick up yards on our regular option plays.

The best to run it? Kitrick Taylor, because he was like a running back playing wide receiver. He could really motor with it.

GO VANDALS!

During some of those frigid Novembers, the University of Idaho's Kibbie Dome provided welcome salvation. Those were the days before so many programs had indoor practice facilities. I truly believe that going over and practicing in the Kibbie Dome when the weather was awful was the key to us being ready to beat Washington in the Apple Cups of 1982 and '83. I know we wouldn't have been nearly as well prepared without the cooperation of the people at Idaho.

Sometimes we had to juggle the schedule around a little bit to make it work, but the kids—heck, the coaching staff, too— really appreciated being able to get in good work-outs without worrying about picking up a case of frostbite or a nasty cold.

One of the worst developments in recent years, to my mind, is when the Cougars started scheduling Idaho again. The reason I never wanted to play them was because, without the on-field competition, it allowed our coaches and their coaches to spend a lot of time together swapping ideas. Dennis Erickson had a great staff over there, and we spent hours talking to John L. Smith, and Gregg Smith and Keith Gilbertson, along with Dennis, of course. We used to look at tapes of each other's offenses. As soon as you have them on the schedule, you can't do that.

I guess I can admit this, but we stole—with their permission, of course—a lot of Dennis's offense. Some of that stuff Dennis was doing with the early passing attack out of the one-back set was really creative and it was very beneficial to a lot of the things we were doing with Mark Rypien. That year we had the RPMs—Mark Rypien, Kerry Porter and Rueben Mayes— a lot of that passing package was Dennis's stuff, and it really was a nice addition to our option package. Hey, if you've got a resource that valuable only eight miles away, you'd be stupid not to exploit it.

GOOD SCOUTS

Most fans have no concept of the contribution made by the guys who don't play on Saturday. They have no earthly idea how much effort it takes to get that team on the field and ready to play. The guys who have so much to do with it, the assistant coaches and the "preparation troops," are never in the spotlight.

A lot of times your success in a game is dependent on how hard and well the scout team prepared you during the week. It was so important to us that we gave awards to the offensive and defensive scout team Player of the Week. On occasion, if they did a great job and had worked hard, we might let them out of sprints. You tried to do different things to show your appreciation.

A couple of the best scout guys we ever had were talents who were redshirting and would go on to be great players for us. Mark Rypien redshirted one year and he was excellent on the scout team. Probably the best we ever had was Samoa Samoa because he'd play whatever position you had, not just quarterback. He loved to play with the defense's mind and he competed so hard that it kept the defense on its toes. Those guys knew that Samoa would make them look bad if they gave him a chance.

One of the fun things for scout-team guys, who saw it as something of an honor, was to be picked to wear the jersey number of an opponent's star player. We would give certain guys the jersey number of an opposing stud because we had to work on the various ways we would key on that guy in the game. A guy might get a star's jersey number for the whole week. It was a badge of honor, and they'd try to emulate, as much as they could, how that guy played. I'll tell you, they took it very seriously; they knew it was important. Even if most of the fans never saw it.

MANY HATS

If I had it to do over again, I'd have phased myself out of the play-calling and spent more time managing the game. I used to be offensive coordinator, quarterbacks coach, head coach and play-caller… all in one afternoon.

A lot of times I'd find I was too caught up in the offense and not thinking as much as I should about game management. I think you can sometimes win games by having a better feeling for the entire game, who is hot, how the momentum is going, when to take chances. Come Saturday night, man, I was drained. That's a lot of thinking and worrying.

WALDENISM

I never held the belief that the quarterback should be treated differently. If they needed to be yelled at, I yelled at them. When a quarterback does something drastically wrong, it's no different than a guard pulling in the wrong direction. If you're going to chew out the guard, you better chew out the quarterback. I think the other players appreciated seeing the quarterback getting his butt chewed, too. It's more democratic.

CHAPTER 17

CHARACTERS, HEROES AND QUOTABLES

HARRY, CHARLIE AND ME

I loved the media when I was at Washington State; we'd have a press conference and then the three of us would go to lunch. That pretty much fulfilled my media obligations. Of course, it got more involved as time went on. But for a while, there, it would just be Harry Missildine and Charlie Van Sickel coming down from the Spokane papers, and whoever would come up that day from the Lewiston *Tribune*.

It was different, then, of course. Harry and Charlie were from a time when you covered the team and then wrote about what good happened. They were more a part of the team than being critics of it. You always knew, no matter what we did, even if we got beat, you might see mention of how good our receivers looked.

The media members from Seattle were always good to me, too. I think they all understood and appreciated that I tried to help them do their jobs. I think I understood what they were doing from the journalism and speech classes I took in college.

Being from the South, I always thought it was important that I learned to use the language correctly and be comfortable speaking.

I don't think enough coaches understand what the sports media is all about, and how much it can help them if they work at the relationship. Of course, these days, it's a lot more than just Harry and Charlie and I heading off for lunch.

JERRY SAGE, HERO

Certainly one of the most impressive and inspirational men I ever had the privilege of meeting while coaching at Washington State was a true war hero and former Cougar, Colonel Jerry Sage. In the mid-80s, Sage came to Pullman for a signing of his autobiography: *SAGE: The Man the Nazis Couldn't Kill.*

Sage was an end out of Spokane's North Central High, who was so well respected by his teammates he was named Cougar captain in 1938, and was so accomplished in the class room that he graduated as a Phi Beta Kappa student.

In 1941, after leaving WSU, Sage reported to the U.S. Army recruiter and brashly announced: "I think we've got to stop this Hitler clown." Sage would do more than his part. He became an Office of Strategic Services (OSS) agent trained in "silent kill" tactics, was captured by the Germans, and attempted so many escapes as a POW it's said that he was the inspiration for the Steve McQueen role in the movie *The Great Escape.* His actual feats were far more impressive than those the movie portrayed, however.

Sage was given the code name "Dagger," and was turned loose with one mission: Get behind the German lines and hurt the enemy any way he could. He and his unit blew up locomo-

This Cougar not only looks tough, he was one of the most famous heroes of World War II. Jerry Sage of Spokane was one of our first OSS agents and broke out of German POW camps so many times he was the inspiration for the Steve McQueen character in The Great Escape. *(Photo courtesy of Washington State University)*

tives, railroads and gasoline dumps in North Africa. But when he took shrapnel from an artillery shell in his leg and shoulder, he was captured by some of Rommel's Afrika Corps. And within his first day as a prisoner, Sage attempted an escape.

At some point in his 15 trips to solitary confinement (the cooler), Sage earned the nickname The Cooler King, the same name given to McQueen's character in the *The Great Escape*. Of the movie and McQueen's role, Sage said: "I didn't do everything McQueen did in the movie. But he didn't do everything I did in real life, either."

Although he had helped in the preparation of the three tunnels that were to make possible the famed Great Escape, Sage was transferred out of Stalag III before the historic break-

out. It was probably fortunate for him, as 50 of the unsuccess-
ful escapees were executed by the Germans. As the war neared
its end, Sage was being moved between camps and managed to
sneak away for the final time. He made his way through
Poland and ultimately back into Allied hands.

Sage won about every honor possible, and after 30 years in
the service, he became a high school teacher. Not one to do
things sparingly, or without distinction, he was named South
Carolina Teacher of the Year in 1979.

One of our assistant coaches, Jon Fabris, heard he was
coming to campus and decided we had to get this guy to talk
to our team. At the time, he was in his late 60s, but he was still
a very imposing man. He called up two of our biggest guys and
asked them to attack him. They were real reluctant, not
because he was so old, but because they understood that he
really knew his stuff. So, in slow motion, one of them came at
him, and Sage showed how he would have broken his arm and
then used that arm to snap his neck.

Our guys were so inspired by him they went out the next
day and clobbered somebody we probably had no right being
in the game with. What an impressive man and a real hero.
He'd have been a great coach, if he'd wanted. I told our coaches: I wish we could get this guy to talk to the team every week.

WSU'S NO. 1 FAN

I miss Beulah Blankenship. She passed in the winter of
2000, and anybody who was a part of Cougar athletics for
some 30 years knew and loved and was touched by Beulah.

Beulah wasn't just a fan, she was a part of our lives, and was
a meaningful force for all of us. She would knit beautiful quilts
for coaches, and make scrapbooks for us. And she's most

famous, of course, for the hundreds of cookies she would always bake for the teams. I have no idea how much time she spent on these kinds of things, but it was always so greatly appreciated.

She was never one of those busy-body fans who always wanted to be a part of things; she just was always there quietly supporting Cougar teams. She wanted nothing in return, just to show her love for the Cougars. I can't tell you how much we all admired and appreciated her. I feel sorry for the Cougar athletes of these days because they have no idea what a great fan and person they lost when Beulah Blankenship died.

MARK SMAHA

Not to minimize the efforts of all the great assistant coaches I worked with over the years, but the No. 1 most reliable and important guy to me, as a head coach, was trainer Mark Smaha. He was the most vital part of what I had to do as a coach in all the years I was at Washington State.

Mark understood me, and we had a great relationship. He knew how badly certain players were needed on the field, but he also knew we weren't going to force anybody back who wasn't ready to play or who needed to be protected from further injury. I trusted his judgment immensely.

Trainers occupy a critical, but mostly unseen, function with a team. They're involved in treatment and rehabilitation, of course, but they're also the team psychologist and, maybe most importantly, the priest. They hear player confessions all the time. And they walk a thin line on what they can and can't pass on to a coach, and what they can say that's important but won't betray the confession.

Mark was good at reading the temperament of the team, without ever attaching a face or a name to it. He sometimes might tell me that there was a lot of grumbling in the locker room and it might be a good time to fool them a little and back off. He didn't do that much, but when he did, I listened, because he was so trustworthy.

It was so saddening that his departure from Washington State was not accompanied by the dignity his years of service deserved. I think the university rushed to judgment on what it thought was a drug problem but was really a pain problem. The demands of a trainer's job—and you can find this is the case with so many others—are such that they tend to develop terrible backs. That's what it was with Mark. There was an investigation, and it was not a good ending for his relationship with a school that he had loved so much, and that should have been so indebted to him in return. He was truly an excellent trainer who would work 24/7 to help young men heal up. And he was the most important guy, and most reliable, I worked with in my years at Washington State.

THE HISTORIC MR. LINCOLN

The coaches and I felt it was crucial for contemporary Cougars to know about their athletic "forefathers." Sometimes people forget how many great players there have been throughout Washington State's history. We knew we had to find our past, polish it up, and sell it to the players as an example of what can be achieved.

I'd try to bring former players back to talk to the guys, and we made sure coaches made reference to them as much as possible. One of those, certainly, was Keith Lincoln, who went on to a great career as a running back in the pros. Lincoln picked up 349 yards of total offense in one AFL championship game for San Diego. That's unbelievable, and Cougar players needed to hear about that.

We told them about Gail Cogdill and Hugh Campbell and Don Ellingsen and Byron Bailey (one of the greatest Canadian football players of all time) and Clarence Williams and Mel Hein and Glen "Turk" Edwards and Don Paul and Harland Svare and Butch Meeker and so many others.

The greatest thing we could sell these kids was our past, and Keith Lincoln was among the greatest ever at Washington State.

A VALUED PUPIL

Only at Washington State. That was a phrase that arose repeatedly when I was there. Only at Washington State. If there were a set of strange circumstances, it would happen at WSU. If something crazy developed, it involved a Cougar. That's what made it such a colorful and entertaining—and thoroughly unpredictable—place to be.

We once had a placekicker, Mike DeSanto, with only one eye. Stop to think how hard that would be to line up a kick that way. Think how that would affect depth perception and perspective from a distance. But I'll tell you what, it made him keep his head down and concentrate. He was a delightful guy who was a terrific kicker and the kind of kid that everybody loved.

The story got back to me that DeSanto was particularly valuable when he was with guys who had more desire for liquid refreshment than they had money. He would drink his beer about halfway down, pop out his glass eye, drop it in the beer, and go up to the bartender complaining about what he found.

Look, he'd say, there's an eye in my beer and we're all grossed out by it, how about a pitcher for the table to help us get over it. Apparently, bartenders rarely quibbled. Although word got around about his ploy, and bartenders started keeping THEIR eyes out for DeSanto.

LET THERE BE LIGHT

One year the people at ABC asked us if we'd move the kickoff for the Apple Cup back from 1 to 4 p.m. The game was in Pullman, so it was our call. And there wasn't much debate on our part; we could always use the TV money, so we did it.

Right away, the people at Washington went berserk. They always act like they're going to freeze to death any time they have to come to Pullman, or worry that the drive is so much worse going from Seattle to Pullman than it is for us going the other direction. Two of the three most miserable games I've ever played in my life, in terms of weather, were in Seattle. I've never been one to believe that freezing rain running down the back of my neck was a particularly enjoyable experience.

They kept complaining: Oh, it will be dark when the game is finished. Somebody from a Seattle paper called me for a comment about that aspect of the controversy. I said: "Well, I don't know what they do on the west side of the state, but over here whenever it gets dark, we just turn on our lights."

PUT IT IN REVERSE

I was at Iowa State in 1988 when we luckily had an open date on a Saturday when the Cougars were scheduled to play at Illinois. Some of my staff and I rented an RV and headed over to see Dennis Erickson's Cougar team play at Champaign. Dennis was doing a fine job and we were swelling up with pride because we felt so good about how well the Cougars were playing.

We loaded that RV up with food and acted like fans, something we never have the chance to do. We tailgated and filled up on hot dogs and just had a wonderful experience sitting up in the stands with all the Washington State fans. The Cougars beat a real good Illinois team and it was a tremendous effort by a great bunch of guys.

I didn't go in the locker room or anything to congratulate them because that was another man's locker room and another man's team, and you just don't do that. But I was glowing, I was so happy for them.

Well, early the next week, somebody called me and asked what I thought about that team. I said I was proud of them and that people should be sure to support them. Now, I used to fight with the fans in Spokane about not coming down to the games. I never thought we got an appropriate per capita amount of people coming down. For a city of 350,000, there should have been at least 20,000 come down every game.

They used to always talk about how hard the drive was, and complain about the two-lane traffic, and the speed traps in Colfax. In a quote that seemed to take on a life of its own, I said that this Cougar team is so good that "I'd drive backward from Spokane to Pullman to watch a game."

From that time on, fans always bring that up when they want my assessment of the Cougars: "Are these guys good enough that you'd drive backward from Spokane to watch?"

Fact is, almost all of them are these days.

MAKING CONCESSIONS

Nobody was getting fabulously wealthy coaching at Washington State in those early years. But if you were a little creative you could beef up the income on occasion. We heard some of the kids coming to our football camps in the summer complaining that there was no place to eat at night. You know how hungry active kids can get in the evening after dinner.

I got all the coaches' wives together and we pooled some money for supplies, and we started making sandwiches to sell. We'd make 150 or so bologna and cheese or peanut butter and jelly sandwiches a day, and sell them for 50 cents, and also sell pops for a quarter or whatever. Those kids were so happy to be able to get something for late-night snacks that we couldn't make enough of them.

Money was tight in those days, and you'd do what you could do. The assistant coaches split the camp money, anyway, and it turned into a pretty good little money-maker for them. It was a win-win for the kids and the coaches. I'll tell you what, though, only at Washington State would you see the coach's wives lined up making sandwiches for the football camp.

CHOW HOUNDS

Mike and John Dreyer were a couple big linemen out of Coeur d'Alene, Idaho, who proved how much a scholarship can be worth to the parents of athletes. Their parents told me that at every meal, aside from a huge main course and several side dishes and desserts, they put a gallon of milk and a loaf of bread on the table. All gone... everything... every night.

They told me that the savings in groceries alone when the boys were at school allowed them to buy tickets and travel to every one of the Cougar away games to watch their boys play.

BIGGEST OVERACHIEVER

Probably the least athletic kid we ever had who still played great for us was guard Gary Patrick. He was a big, ol' guy out of Yakima who had bad feet and couldn't run very well.

He was always pretty cranky, and what really got him mad was when somebody else would complain about having to run wind sprits. Gary hated running, too, but when somebody would gripe, he'd jump all over them, growling: "Shut up and run."

He was such a tough kid that we loved him dearly. But he wasn't much of an athlete. You tend to think that playing basketball is an example of how athletic a person is. If you asked Gary to play basketball, he'd say something like, "Actually, I'd rather have a hemorrhoid operation."

He was really and truly not a gifted athlete. But here's what he did: he just fired out and clobbered the first person he could get to as hard as he could. He started at least two years for us because he was an ornery guy with a gnarly attitude who just really loved playing football, and refused to recognize any physical limitations. That's just about exactly what you want in an offensive lineman.

WATCHING IS TOUGH

I think I can speak for most coaches, we don't like going to football games unless we have some involvement with one of the teams. Coaches are just too intense, and they don't watch games the way fans do.

I am not good at sitting with fans in the stands because they're always cheering and I'm just busy trying to see what's going on. That's why most coaches who aren't working would rather sit in the press box because there's no cheering allowed up there. They can just sit quietly and enjoy a good view of the action. Fans used to ask me why I wasn't cheering. Heck, I was too busy trying to figure out why the draw play didn't work.

I may be pulling for Washington State, but I'm also going to be interested in what Stanford is doing with its scheme. Coaches are just way too intense to be fans.

WALDENISM

The only thing that really infuriated me was when officials got lazy. I was a basketball official for years when I was a high school football coach, so I knew the importance of hustling and being in position. At times, from the sideline, I could tell when a crew wasn't in tune with the game. Not being biased, nothing to help me or hurt me, but they were hurting the game by not being in position. That smelled of bad officiating, and I hated it because it was unfair to the players.

CHAPTER 18

MO-PEDS AND MOPING AROUND

MO-PED WEEK

We came into the 1986 season with some terrific young talent, but I knew our inexperience was going to give us troubles along the way. We went down to Berkeley to take on California in Strawberry Canyon the third week of the season, and we were more than just young… we were awful.

I didn't mind them making some mistakes, but I could not tolerate the lack of effort I saw that day. We did not do one single thing that was good in that game. I always tried to instill in them the idea that, no matter how good or bad your team is, you can always play hard. That's the rallying cry for the downtrodden, you can always play harder than an opponent. And that should have been enough to beat Cal. Instead, we lost 31-21.

I was furious with our performance and after the game and I made the statement: "I realize there are some Sherman Tanks in this league, but we just got run over by a damned Mo-Ped." At the time I said it, I didn't mean to knock Cal, it's just that they were struggling like we were, and they surely weren't up there with some of the high and mighty teams in the league.

Cal coach Joe Kapp was furious and he called me: "What do you mean comparing my team to a Mo-Ped?" I told him I didn't mean it as an insult, but there it was. I probably shouldn't have said it.

I simply could not allow our team to think it ever could be excused for playing with an effort that poor. So, the next week, I put our team on a death march. If you ask any of those guys about the dreaded Mo-Ped Week, they'll tell you it was like the worst boot camp they could go through. I realized that I did not have their attention, but I surely was going to get it that week.

It was like going back to spring practice; we had live tackling drills, we scrimmaged live, we went first-team offense against first-team defense, we had live goal line, live kicking game. Truthfully, I'm embarrassed about it now, because I never saw myself as being a mean guy. I didn't do it to run anybody off. I just knew we were a lot better than we had played, and this was a group of guys who had to learn how important winning was, and how hard you had to work at Washington State if you were going to beat teams.

It was brutal. But it made them so mad that they took it out against Arizona State the next Saturday, tying them 21-21 on the road. Remember, that was a 10-1-1 Sun Devils team that won the conference and finished ranked No. 4 in the nation. In short, I think it proved they understood the Message of the Mo-Ped. That week, they took on one of the Sherman Tanks and fought it dead even.

Finally, once and for all, I want to apologize to all the guys I put through that. I'm sorry. I shouldn't have done it. I was mad and they paid dearly. I just felt they had to learn that the kind of effort they showed at Cal was never going to be acceptable.

TOUCH DOWN, COUGARS

The pilot came on to tell us that Eugene was socked in and we'd just circle a while until he "found a hole" in the overcast that he could fly through. It didn't sound promising. But after circling for a while, he said, "I think I see a spot… button up and let's go for it." Holy cow, he started bringing us down through the clouds. And we were looking out the window and seeing nothing. Coming down. Seeing nothing. Coming down. Seeing nothing. Man, it's getting nervous in that plane. I mean to tell you, very frightening.

We were straining our eyes out the window, but couldn't see anything but clouds, even though we got that feeling that we had to be getting a lot closer. Just about the moment we thought we could see something, we hit that runway–hard, with stuff flying all over the cabin—and all our kids started screaming like crazy. Our guys said it wasn't a landing as much as it was an "organized crash." When we got off the plane, quarterback Ed Blount caught up to me: "Coach, if it's all right with you, I'm hitch-hiking back to Pullman."

JAMES HASTY

Some things a coach simply doesn't hear very frequently. One of the rarest is a fabulous athlete walking into his office telling him that he'd like to transfer to his school—walk on if he has to—for academic reasons. One day, James Hasty did exactly that, stressing how important it was to his scholastic future that he transfer from Central Washington to Washington State. We offered better classes in his field of study.

Believe me, it didn't take us very long to find a scholarship for a guy with the talent to go on to have a 13-year career in the NFL. Good recruiting on our part, eh? I was certain he was going to be an all-world free safety, but I had no idea he'd be as great a cornerback as he turned into. And not a bad student, either.

THE BRUISER

My early impressions of Steve Broussard were not favorable, and if I'd stayed at Washington State, he probably would have had to leave. I thought he was a lazy kid who had been one of those babied athletes you see sometimes. With him, there was always the strained hamstring or quad or bruised toe. And he seemed to believe you could practice one day a week and then go out and play on Saturday. I never cared for that attitude.

As a reliable back at the time, I liked Michael Pringle much more because he was one tough sucker who would go 100 miles an hour in practice. He was everything in terms of energy and effort that Bruiser wasn't. The fact that Pringle played so well in the Canadian Football League showed how good he was.

But Bruiser certainly turned out to be a great football player, and I have to give Dennis Erickson credit for dealing with him better than I ever did. You could tell the talent was there; he had won the city 100-meter dash championship in Los Angeles, and when you do that, you know you're fast. He had such a low center of gravity that it was almost impossible to knock him off his feet. He just never worked that hard for us, and we always felt you had to earn the right, with your effort in practice, to play in the games on Saturdays.

WALDENISM

Face it, there's no time in history when young people haven't irritated the old people of that time. We might as well understand it and deal with it. I'm sure my players have sons today who are irritating them now. Maybe it shouldn't, but in a way, that delights me.

TIMM ROSENBACH

The easiest recruit I ever had was Timm Rosenbach, who was like a second son to us. He and my son Murray were inseparable at Pullman High... great friends, and they still are. I loved Timm's dad, Lynn, and his mom, Rosie, who were great people to have working at the university.

Timm's talents were a little bit unexplored as he never got to throw the ball much playing for run-oriented Ray Hobbs at Pullman High. But I had an advantage on other college coaches because I'd seen Timm throwing the ball around with Murray for years. Even early on in high school, Timm could throw the ball 60 yards, and he had great body-hand control that made him a super athlete.

A lot of schools saw him as a defensive back—and he could have been a fierce free safety—but I really understood how well he could throw the ball. We wanted him badly, of course, and we told him he should just stay at home and we'd let him play quarterback.

He didn't get to play much when he first joined us, and then he kind of got thrown into the fire when Dennis Erickson took over after I left. I know he got flustered trying to learn the system. But give Dennis a lot of credit for knowing how much substance there was with Timmy, because he stayed with him. That next year it surely paid off with a fabulous season.

MIKE UTLEY

I chewed on Mike Utley as forcefully as anybody I ever coached. He had worked his way down to his final chance to stay at Washington State.

He had been a big, ol' kid out of Kennedy High in Seattle, maybe 6-6, 250, but he seemed only so-so as a football player. Assistant coach Gary Gagnon really liked him, but he knew I wasn't quite sold on him. You almost don't want to admit something like this, because you can't allow yourself to think this way, but I kind of wondered why Washington wasn't after him. I went over with Gary to take a look at him playing basketball. He had a broken arm at the time, but you know, he moved up and down pretty well, had good feet and really got after it even with his arm in a cast. I knew then he'd be fine if he wanted to work at it.

So we took him. But when he got to campus, I'll tell you, he was a loose cannon. He liked to party... so much so that he was not going to make it academically. I brought him in and really got after him. I confess, I said some terrible things to him to try to get his attention and let him know how much he was throwing away. I had heard him saying he wanted to play in the NFL; I told him he'd never have the chance at the rate he was going. I never wanted to give up on anybody, I told him, but I was almost there with him.

If he missed another class the rest of the semester—just one class—he'd be run off on the spot because he was wasting everybody's time. "I believe you can be a wonderful NFL player, but you'll be nothing if you don't become a man and have

Quarterback Timm Rosenbach always appreciated the protection of Mike Utley. Both of these Cougs went on to the NFL, where Mike suffered a tragic injury. The way he's worked for research and funding for projects to benefit those with spinal injuries has been truly inspiring. (Photo courtesy of Washington State University)

the guts and discipline to show up to class and live up to your responsibilities," I told him.

He later told me that the confrontation made him realize that it was all about to head down the tubes, and he understood his only options were to go to class or go home. You know what... he shaped up. It's like that story where sometimes you've just got to whack them to get their attention.

Give him all the credit from that point, because he really decided to mature, and I never had one speck of trouble.

The one thing I knew for certain was that he'd be a great pro player, because he so loved the competition. There was a fire inside him to play football. When he was injured and paralyzed while playing for the Detroit Lions, it broke my heart. It was so terrible to see his career cut short because I knew he was a man who lived for the game, who had the most ferocious competitiveness. To think that that light was going to go out just broke my heart.

But you know what... it didn't go out. I don't know that I've ever been so proud of a man as I have been of Mike Utley. It is unbelievable the things he's done, and the ways in which he's helped other people. He went back to school; he's skiing and doing all sorts of things. That terrible accident has never stopped him. To see how he competes against his circumstances, to see the way he's dealt with that devastating injury, has been the most courageous thing. To me, that man is a hero.

TIM PETEK

In my first season as head coach, Spud Harris died suddenly on the field. In my last season, we went through the prolonged agony of the passing of another wonderful guy. Tim Petek, a defensive lineman out of Gonzaga Prep, had been starting and playing a lot for us. At his young age, for no earthly reason, he was stricken with lung cancer. Here was a powerful young man, 250 pounds, who just got sicker and sicker. We wanted to keep him involved with the program as much as possible, and made sure he came to practice whenever he felt like it to keep his spirits up. But to see what this disease was doing to him physically was so upsetting. He put up a courageous fight to beat this disease, and we all gained perspective from his brave battle.

APPLE CUP '86: DISAPPOINTMENT

I can't tell you how hard it is to come off the field and know that your team did not compete. It was the first time in an Apple Cup game since 1978 that I felt we didn't show up ready to compete. I'll take the blame for that. I can tell you, that game didn't do much for my emotional stability.

It had been nine years, and I felt that we had not only leveled the field with those guys, we had it tipped in our direction for a while. And then to see it slipping was very disheartening. We lost 44-23 at home in a game that sent me a message. Maybe Washington State needs a change; maybe Jim Walden needs a change. Sometimes there are signs that maybe the players aren't buying what you're selling anymore. Or maybe you're just not selling it well enough anymore.

I could not understand why the team wasn't playing better, but I had to look at myself. Maybe I wasn't happy about some off-the-field things, and they picked up on that. To me, that's an unforgivable thing for a coach to do to his players. You can't have your problems becoming their problems. They're here to play, not to have to worry about their coach.

We were up 10-7 early in the game, but Chris Chandler threw four touchdown passes and we never did much to battle back. That ballgame as much as came out and screamed at me that it was time to go. I'm not so sure I made a great choice in where to go, but I think it was the right thing to go. I had never really envisioned leaving Washington State. And I knew this was going to turn into a really good team. But that game convinced me the team might benefit from playing for somebody else.

CHAPTER 19

ON AIR

A HOMER... YOU BET

I don't try to kid anybody, when I'm in that broadcast booth working the Cougar games, I'm not neutral. I'm pulling for Washington State all the way. Am I a homer? Yep. Is that a bad thing? I don't know and I don't care. I'm not trying to get a job with ESPN, so I don't care if somebody complains that I'm not neutral. Harry Caray loved the Cubs... seems like that worked okay. So, I want the Cougars to win, and I'm not up there to try to second-guess Bill Doba or Mike Price. But I am up there to try to be analytical and tell the fans just what happened and why.

Coaches in the broadcast booth have trouble with getting too technical. My son Murray is my sounding board on that. He'll listen and tell me afterward that I can't tell listeners that the defensive tackle was in a "3 technique," but that he was lined up on the outside shoulder of the guard.

And, so far, I've been able to remember when my mic is on so I haven't said too many bad words. My association with KXLY has been a wonderful thing. I have really enjoyed it and it's been one of the most fun things I've ever done. I don't know if anybody else likes it… but I do.

BOB ROBERTSON

I describe Cougar broadcaster Bob Robertson as the ultimate professional. His voice is the sound of Cougar football for so many thousands of fans. He describes football action as well as anybody I've ever known.

What I love most is the way he works for both teams. A lot of play-by-play guys can tell you all about their team, but when the other team has the ball they might as well be talking about tulips. Bob knows what's going on with both sides of the field. I really feel privileged to be in the booth with somebody I respect so much.

We're both talkative guys, of course, and the listener isn't going to get much out of it if we're both yakking at the same time. At first, it was a little hard because Bob sometimes doesn't like to give up the microphone. He was conditioned that way because he spent so much time doing his own color without an analyst in the booth. When you do that, you had better have a pretty long list of things to talk about. There's 22 seconds of time to kill between plays and you'd better be able to fill the time. Bob had to get used to that.

Most play-by-play guys don't know much about the game of football. They can describe the things they see unfolding on the field. They will tell you that the fullback ran the ball up the middle. But most of them can't tell you it was a trap play, and why they called it, and why it worked or didn't work against that defense. That's my job. And if I can provide that information in a colorful way, or attach an interesting story to it, all the better.

What I have to make sure I do is give Bob as much space as he needs. And at first, it was tough to get my six seconds in. But these are long broadcasts and there's going to be plenty of time to say all I need. The fact is, it's up to me to adjust to Bob because I'm in his world. I'm not coaching, this is broadcasting, he's the pro in this field. I think he trusts me more now to say something that adds to the broadcast.

I hope that when he leaves that booth after every game that he's happy with the broadcast. He's earned the right to feel that every broadcast was a good one. I may interrupt him sometimes when he's talking about somebody's grandfather and I want to talk about a post-corner route. But he's truly wonderful at what he does. He's the best, in fact.

SEEN ONE, SEEN 'EM ALL

A distressing sameness has taken over college football. As I watch the game as it's evolved, it makes me think that the NFL has finally taken over. I always felt that college football's greatness was in its flexibility, its diversity of schemes and styles. Some teams ran four-man or five-man fronts on defense. The offenses would be wishbone, veer, the I, three-wides, two-tights. Every week was a potpourri of offenses and mindsets, things you had to adjust to as a coach.

Now, discouragingly, every football coach in America is running the exact same thing. There's not more than 10 percent variance between the offenses you see from week to week. With the exception of Air Force, Navy and Nebraska, the other 109 Division I schools are doing the one-back, three-wides offense. Tendencies may be different, but the alignments and plays are mostly the same.

Once upon a time, in the course of an 11-week season, you'd see two wishbones, two veers, an I triple-option... there might be six dramatically different packages you had to prepare for during a season. Now, it's all pass-and-catch, and Cover 2 or man coverage. It's so simple that even the fans fully understand what's going on. For the first time, fans can now shout stuff from the stands that they actually know.

WALDENISM

Coaches get caught up in their world as being the most important thing there is. I never felt that was the case. The game this Saturday is not among the top 20 of the world's problems. It's important to us, sure, and to the people who are watching it. But coaching football is not a cure for cancer. As much as some might not want to believe it, there's billions of people who somehow manage to get up in the morning without even taking a peek at the sports page.

CHAPTER 20

OTHER COUGARS

DREW BLEDSOE

Drew Bledsoe starred at Washington State in that span after I left as coach and before I returned in the broadcast booth. I feel a little deprived that I didn't get the opportunity to see him develop. It seems to me he is an amalgam of all the positive things you can say about so many of the great Cougar players for so many years. He was so much like Rueben Mayes and Jack Thompson and others… people with great family backgrounds who were great people in their own right, and, of course, fabulous athletes.

I know that Drew has represented the university at the highest level and continues to do so. You're not surprised when a guy who has that much character to go along with so much talent is successful on the big stage.

Beyond that, he's an example of the incredible legacy there's been at Washington State and, heck, at Washington, too, with quarterbacks produced in the state. Trace them back on our side with Drew and Timm Rosenbach and Mark

Quarterback Drew Bledsoe was one of the great Cougars I didn't get a chance to coach, but he certainly represents so many of the great things about the Washington State football program. (Photo courtesy of Washington State University)

Rypien and Clete Casper and Jack Thompson, and on the Huskies' side with the Huards, Steve Pelleur, Billy Joe Hobert, Tom Flick... what an unbelievable legacy for a state. As impressive as that list is, Drew may have been the best of them all.

RYAN LEAF

I have never seen one guy mishandled worse as a pro quarterback than Ryan Leaf. I don't think he always handled his situation in the most mature manner, either, but it still seems that he was a talented kid who got a bad rap.

When you're the second player taken in the draft as a quarterback, believe me, you're not going to a good team. Those are the facts. And it's my opinion that the San Diego Chargers did as bad a job handling the pressure Leaf was going to face as the Indianapolis Colts did a good job in protecting Peyton Manning.

The Chargers had about two good players at the time, but they threw this high-strung kid out there, a kid with probably more confidence than he needed, and let him get eaten alive. They pulled him out of a sick-bed in Kansas City to play in a terrible rainstorm, to suffer through a four-interception game... and he was never the same after that.

After he had that confrontation with a reporter, he was seen as the bad boy of the NFL. I think it was a horse crap thing and they never did much to protect him or help him. I think the whole Ryan Leaf saga in the NFL was badly handled from the start. On his side, he didn't handle the rejection well. But I think the organization just threw away a great athlete and a terrific Cougar quarterback.

JASON GESSER

You couldn't help but love watching Jason Gesser play; he brought so much heart and competitiveness to the game. Although I think I loved hearing him talk almost as much as watching him play. He's got that Hawaiian dialect, and whenever he spoke I always thought I was listening to Samoa Samoa.

The uncanny thing, and what spoke so much about his character, was how much his teammates respected him. It made him a tremendous leader. I saw in him so many of the same qualities of the great leaders Washington State has had over time: He was highly competitive, with good skills and a terrific personality.

I don't know if people truly understand what he accomplished at UCLA in the last game of 2002. It was crucial… they needed it to get to the Rose Bowl, and there was Gesser playing with his ankle in a cast to protect a painful injury.

Forever and ever, Jason Gesser's performance in that game has to be one of the greatest individual efforts of overcoming pain and injury. To see him do that is absolutely off the charts in terms of sacrifices an individual can make for his team. On the road, in Pasadena, in a game they had to win… to quarterback with one foot was a stunning achievement.

I would rank that as the No. 1 courageous Cougar effort of all time.

MARCUS TRUFANT

When I got back in the broadcast booth working the Cougar games on radio, one of the first things that just jumped out at me so unmistakably was this kid, Marcus Trufant, who was an incredible cornerback.

I don't know that I had seen anybody like him; nobody had the footwork and covered as quietly as he did. It was as if he had James Hasty's body with Ricky Reynolds' feet. I thought, man, this guy can really cover. I immediately knew that this was a kid who had what it takes to become not just an NFL cornerback, but one of the great NFL cornerbacks.

CHAPTER 21

A TIME TO GO

SAYING GOODBYE

December always brought sadness. It was the end of a season, and the end of a commitment. It was the last time that particular team, with all the components that combined to make it special and different from all the others, would be together.

You spend four or five years with these kids, and when they're seniors, it's hard to let them go. You know their good qualities, and you have a special story about every one of them. You've been a big part of each others' lives.

What you come to realize is that you never have enough time to just put your arms around them while you've got them. You're so busy and they're so busy, and you're always afraid somebody will think you've got favorites, so you get cautious. You may be together over the course of four or five years, but there's just never enough time with them.

You see many of them later, of course, but they've moved on. I am thankful that, as far as I know, I've only lost one former player. John Winslow was a gifted athlete from Shawnee Mission, Kansas, who was an all-world defensive player with an interest in becoming a Cougar. It was a dream situation where he was a great player we didn't even know about, but who had ties to Washington State and just wanted to be a Cougar. It turned out that his grandparents lived in Colfax. He was just a joy to us. He died in an automobile accident in the Chelan area. It's such a hard thing to believe.

It's tough to see any of them leave. I believe that the hardest thing for a coach to do is go through that last game because you fall in love with every one of those guys and you just never want to have to say goodbye.

THE URGE FOR GOING

Frankly, if I had it to do over again, I wouldn't have gone to Iowa State. They had just been placed on probation by the NCAA and been hit with scholarship sanctions. There also were some things that were promised that never happened. I'd have either stayed at Washington State another couple years or picked another school to try. Had I waited two weeks longer, I probably would have been the head coach at Arizona. I was offered the opportunity, but it had been only two weeks since I had agreed to the Iowa State job, and I wouldn't change my mind at that point. Of course, with Arizona being in the conference, I also had a hard time envisioning having to coach against Washington State every year.

There wasn't really one reason for me to leave WSU. It wasn't coaching that got me out of there. And whatever happened certainly didn't diminish my love for the place. I just felt that maybe they needed some new blood, that it was time they heard a new voice. I had spent nine years battling to stay above

I loved Washington State so much that it was pretty hard keeping my emotions together when I announced I was leaving for Iowa State. The media was used to it, though, as I'd cry at the drop of a hanky. (Photo courtesy of Washington State University)

.500, battling the budget, battling to improve the facilities. At some point, you feel like you should stop the battling. But, of course, I could never see myself doing that.

We had a new president, Sam Smith, a wonderful person who became a great president. He brought in three new associate vice presidents, none of whom knew a thing about me. I had a new athletic director, and Dick Young was fine. But I didn't feel as comfortable as I had felt with the people who brought me in and had grown with me. I saw some things changing, and I worried that I was becoming an irritant to everybody. I thought I was probably wearing thin on them. Heck, I was wearing thin on myself. In my own heart, I was tired of fighting, but didn't know how to stop it.

While there wasn't really any one thing, one of the last things that got me upset came at the start of the 1986 season. We had spent the summer talking with fans about making game day a whole-day experience. Come early, tailgate, have parties like they do just about everywhere else in the country. Make a day out of it. Bring your grill, have a party. Well, what goes along with that? Sure, you're going to have a beer or a glass of wine.

But at our first home game, the campus cops were out there writing tickets to people who were doing exactly what we had told them to do. No drinking, blah, blah, blah. We spent the whole summer trying to get people to come and make a party out of it and when they do, they get ticketed for it. By Monday, I had 50 calls from people asking me what was going on. I felt responsible.

It made me mad and very frustrated. That sort of thing never quit, and it wore on me. I loved the place and I still do, that hasn't diminished a bit. But in my heart, I felt it was time for them to have a new coach. In the end I knew without a doubt that I left the program better than I found it. I'm proud of that.

Of course, as I tend to do, I got emotional when I made the announcement. I was never ashamed of crying in front of people. I told the media not to make too much of it, though, because I cry just watching *Lassie* reruns.

BEING A COUGAR

I can't define it; I can't tell somebody who isn't a Cougar what it's like. There's something that happens at Washington State, you quietly and subtly become infected. There are very few people I've ever met who have gone to WSU and not come away with a favorable impression.

In my case, it first was an opportunity. They gave me a chance. And then they were tolerant and they were respectful and they were appreciative. I loved every minute of living in Pullman. I loved being a Washington State employee. I even loved the battles we had to fight to keep it moving forward. Somehow, it just grows on you.

I have to be honest, at no time in my eight years at Iowa State was I ever as much of a Cyclone. I never really was. I coached there, yes. I worked there. But that was a job. Washington State was a passion. Being a Cougar was a passion.

WALDENISM

There's a story about a preacher and a farmer. The preacher rides up and sees the farmer hard at work on a piece of ground.

The preacher tells the farmer: "You and the Lord have done a great job getting most of those bushes and thorns cleared off the land."

The farmer looked back and said: "Yes padre, pretty good. There's more to do, but you should have seen how bad it looked when the Lord had it all to himself."

That's kind of how I felt at Washington State. There may have been a few thorns and bushes still to be cleared when I left, but, man, you should have seen what it looked like when I got it.